POLLUTERS PAY

The Control of Pollution Act Explained

by

R. Macrory, M.A., of Grays Inn, Barrister,

and

B. Zaba, B.Sc., Ph.D.
Research Biochemist, University of North Wales

Friends of the Earth is an environmental pressure group funded by voluntary contributions. It has over 200 local groups in the UK and is part of a world-wide federation of similar organisations. FoE actively pursues campaigns on energy strategy, transport policy, the use of land, the protection of endangered species and the use of material resources. FoE is associated with the environmental research charity Earth Resources Research.

British Library Cataloguing in Publication Data
Macrory, R
    Polluters Pay.
    1. Great Britain. Laws, statutes, etc.
    (Individual titles). Control of Pollution Act 1974.
    2. Pollution — Great Britain.
    I. Title   II. Zaba, B   III. Friends of the Earth
    344'.41'0463   KD3372.A3/

ISBN 0-905966-11-2

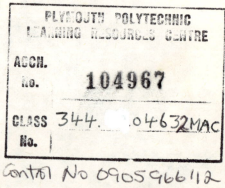
Published by   Friends of the Earth Ltd., 9 Poland Street, London W1V 3DG
Copyright   © Friends of the Earth Ltd., 1978
                 ISBN 0 905966 11 2
Cover design   by Reg Boorer
Printed by   Robendene (Chesham) Ltd.

CONTENTS

INTRODUCTION

PART V: GENERAL POWERS

HOW TO USE *POLLUTER PAYS*

1. *Polluters Pay* follows the main divisions of the 1974 Control of Pollution Act — LAND, WATER, NOISE and AIR.
   Each section contains an introduction which briefly explains the legal context of the new provisions. This is followed by explanations of the main provisions of the Act, together with advice on action that could be taken by individuals or groups (in **bold**).

2. The legal explanations are not intended to be a substitute for an annotated legal guide for practitioners (other books do that) but they should give anyone a reasonable understanding of the law; it is worthwhile reading these sections in conjunction with a copy of the Act itself (£1.70 from Her Majesty's Stationery Office).

3. The sections in **bold** are in no way a comprehensive guide to all the opportunities created by the Act: practical experience will no doubt reveal many more.

4. As any lawyer knows, the difference between 'may' and 'must' in a Statute is crucial. The same is true throughout this guide, and when approaching Authorities, you must be quite clear whether the section of the Act in question has imposed on them a discretion or a duty.

5. The Act received Royal Assent in 1974, but has been brought into force in stages. This makes it particularly difficult for the layman trying to understand the legal implications, and it is important to note carefully whether or not a Commencement Order for the Section in question or regulations have yet been issued.

6. Frequent references are made in the text of *Polluters Pay* to Sections of the 1974 Control of Pollution Act, these appear as *Section 2, s.2* or *s.2(3) (a)* and should not be confused with references to paragraphs within *Polluters Pay* which appear as 2.6 or 4.3.

Introduction

This country has a long history of legal controls over pollution, ranging from old common law remedies such as the action for nuisance to a mass of complicated statutes introduced on an ad hoc basis over the past 150 years. But the Control of Pollution Act 1974 represents a major development: it is the first attempt in the United Kingdom to legislate comprehensively on the subject of environmental pollution. This is an important achievement. But on top of this throughout the Act runs the theme that the general public should have far greater access than before to information on pollution, and a greater chance to influence decisions on pollution control. These decisions may be about specific sources of pollution. But they will also concern longer-term strategic plans affecting the environment, which authorities now have the power and sometimes the duty to establish.

The law can be a powerful weapon in the fight against pollution, and the aim of this guide is to explain to the general public the main effect of the new legislation and the opportunities it has created. In doing so, we hope to increase the confidence and effectiveness of anyone who is concerned with environmental issues.

Acknowledgements: Many thanks to all our colleagues at Poland Street for their assistance, and especially David Pedley and Mike Hudson who both spent several laborious hours proof-reading.
A first draft of the guide was tested in the field by a large number of local Friends of the Earth groups, and their experience and comments proved invaluable. We are also grateful to the Department of the Environment who kindly checked through the first draft for accuracy, though we must take responsibility for the final version of the text.

RM/BZ

The title **'Polluters Pay'** *is derived from the principle, officially adopted by E.E.C. member countries in 1973: namely, that he who creates the pollution should be financially responsible for controlling it. The implications of the principle are not without controversy, especially as some have interpreted it to mean a right to create pollution provided you can pay for it; neither the EEC Commission nor ourselves subscribe to such an interpretation.*

PART I: LAND

Sections 1–30

INTRODUCTION

1.1 This part of the Act is concerned mainly with the collection and disposal of household, commercial and industrial waste. The provisions control both the routine disposal of material collected by local authorities and commercial operators, and the disposal of dangerous and poisonous wastes. Sites on which waste is to be deposited have long been subject to planning controls since they require planning permission from the local authority under the Town and Country Planning Acts[1], and, in addition, a number of laws on Public Health deal with specific pollution caused by the deposit of waste. But the existing legislation was found inadequate to deal with bad dumping practices[2], and following the discovery of cyanide dumping in the Midlands by a local amenity group, the Deposit of Poisonous Waste Act 1972 (see below 1.20) was hastily introduced as a stop-gap measure to control the dumping of particularly poisonous substances.

The Control of Pollution Act introduces for the first time an overall system of control on the deposit of waste in Great Britain; the day-to-day running of the scheme is kept very much in the hands of local authorities, but the new provisions should provide greater conformity and higher standards than before.

WASTE DISPOSAL PLANS

Section 2
Commencement Order S.1. 1977/2164
Regulations Issued   Not Yet

1.2 A criticism of the previous law was the lack of provisions for strategic planning of waste disposal. *Section 2* of the Act now obliges DISPOSAL AUTHORITIES (County or Greater London Councils) to undertake a SURVEY in their area, in order to assess what arrangements are needed for the disposal of household, industrial and commercial waste (known throughout the Act as 'Controlled Waste')[3], which is already in the area and which is likely to arise in the future.

---

(1) All new sites still require planning permission; other activities involving the deposit of waste may not need planning permission (cf s.22(3)(b) Town & Country Planning Act 1971 and General Development Order 1973).

(2) Report of Working Party on Waste Disposal (HMSO – DOE Circular 26/71).

(3) The Act does not cover MINING, QUARRYING, AGRICULTURAL or RADIO-ACTIVE wastes, though in the Waste Management Papers the DOE has advised Disposal Authorities to include these types of wastes in the Survey and Plan.

1.3 Following the initial Survey, the Disposal Authority must prepare a WASTE DISPOSAL PLAN, a strategic document including information on:
   (i) the kinds and quantities of waste with which the Authority expects to deal
   (ii) the methods to be used for its disposal
   (iii) the sites and equipment to be used
   (iv) the estimated cost of these operations.

1.4 In preparing the Waste Disposal Plan, the Disposal Authority is obliged to consult the local Water Authorities (see 2.3), the District or London Borough Councils in its area (known in this Part of the Act as COLLECTION AUTHORITIES), any other Disposal Authority who might be affected by the Plan, and any other persons whom the Authority considers to be representative of those 'engaged by way of trade or business in the disposal of controlled waste' *(s.2(3)(a))*. In addition, the Secretary of State may prescribe by regulations other persons who must be consulted. *(s.2(3)(a)(vi))*.

Before finalizing the Plan, the Disposal Authority must publicize a DRAFT PLAN for public consultation, consider any representations made by members of the public, and make changes where it considers appropriate *(s.2(3)(b))*. The Authority must then send a copy of the final plan to the Secretary of State, and ensure that the plan is given adequate publicity in its area.

1.5 **The Waste Disposal Plan is seen as an important strategic document, and Local Authorities have been advised by the Department of the Environment that the initial Survey and Plan should look forward over a period of ten years. The Plan will have important implications for the environment in a county, since it will involve many policy options (especially whether to dispose of waste by reclamation or by 'land-fill'), all of which will have an effect on the local amenity in different ways. Local Groups should do all they can to influence the scope and content of the Plans, and there are opportunities for this at several stages in the process:-**

1.6 **Initial Surveys: Before *Section 2* came into force, the Department of the Environment advised local authorities that there was nothing to stop them embarking on the Survey on controlled waste in their area. The Department has issued a guidance paper [1], and many local authorities have already completed these Surveys[2]. You should find out first whether your Disposal Authority has made the Survey yet.**

(1) Waste Management Paper No. 2, Waste Disposal Surveys (HMSO 1976).

(2) As of June 1978, one third of Disposal Authorities has completed their Surveys. Of the remainder, over a half had commenced the Surveys. For further details, cf DOE Circular 29/78.

The Authority is not obliged to publish the findings of the Survey (unlike the Waste Disposal Plan), but since it will provide the raw data for the Plan, you should contact the Authority at once, if you feel they may have overlooked some important considerations, such as a large recycling centre run by your group.

1.7   Draft Plans: You will be able to make representations when the Draft Plan is eventually published, but clearly you are likely to have far more influence on the content of the final Plan if you are consulted during preparation of the Draft Plan. Legally, the Disposal Authority must consult those it considers to be representative of persons "engaged by way of trade or business in the disposal of controlled waste", and it is possible that a group operating a reasonably large paper collection scheme might be included in that section. But there is, of course, nothing to prevent the Authority going beyond its statutory duty to consult certain persons, and, if you have already been in contact with the Authority about the Survey, you may well be able to have some influence here. The key is to have made yourself known to the Authority at an early stage.

You should find out from the Disposal Authority its time-table for completing the Survey and Draft Plan, and try to ensure that you are consulted during the preparation of the Plan.

Once the Draft Plan is published, members of the public have an opportunity to make representations, and you should send in written comments at this stage, especially if you have had little success in influencing the contents of the Draft Plan. A well-argued paper should receive good local press, and win local support. An ambitious group could even produce an 'alternative' Draft Plan and this again would attract publicity and might win the support of Councillors.

1.8   Reclamation of waste: The recycling and reclamation of waste could be issues of great importance in the final Waste Disposal Plans, and Section 2 of the Act twice makes specific reference to the subject.

(1) A Waste Disposal Authority, in preparing its Plan (and any subsequent modifications that are relevant) MUST consider, in consultation with those it thinks appropriate, 'what arrangements can reasonably be expected to be made for the purpose of reclaiming substances' from waste in its area (*s.2(4) (a)*) and 'what provisions should be included in the Plan for that purpose' (*s.2(4) (b)*).

(2) The Plan itself MUST include information on the methods for disposing of waste in the area 'either by reclaiming substances from it or otherwise' (*s.2(2) (e)*).

The upshot of this is that the Disposal Authority must at least consider the subject of reclamation seriously (and probably make specific mention of it in the Plan, if only to reject the method as a serious option). If you are interested in the subject, you should make sure that the Authority discuss the issue on a realistic basis.[1] Find out from the Authority how they intend to exercise their duty of considering the subject (*s.2(4) (a)*), and where your group has had some experience of recycling, you ought to be able to persuade the Authority that it should consider you 'appropriate' for consultation under this section. This may be particularly important to achieve, where you have failed to persuade the Authority that you are 'representative of those engaged by way of trade or business in the disposal' of waste, and therefore entitled to be consulted generally on the drafting of the Plan (c.f. 1.5 and 1.7 above).

Some groups might be able to discuss with the Authority the practicalities of recycling schemes, and other issues that could be examined include, (i) the inefficiency of totally voluntary recycling schemes (ii) the desirability of segregating waste at source (iii) publicity for recycling schemes and the use of public collection points for such schemes (iv) the publication of local 'waste directories', giving information of where different types of waste can be recycled in the local area (v) the authorization of members of the public to help themselves from local authority skips, as a way of encouraging 'personal recycling'[2].

The scope for ideas is wide, but the effect you will have on the contents of the Waste Disposal Plan will largely depend on how you present your arguments. A Disposal Authority is not obliged to consult with you, and even if it does, it does not have to include any of your proposals in the Plan. You should therefore always act with politeness, though the stronger the contents of your ideas and the wider their public support, the more you can afford to be firm at the same time.

1.9 **Revisions of the Plan:** The Department of the Environment have suggested that Waste Disposal Plans and initial Surveys should look forward for a period of ten years (the Act is silent on this point), but under *s.2(1) (d)* and *(e)*, the Disposal Authority may 'from time to time' make further Surveys and modifications to the Plan, as they think appropriate. In preparing any modification, the Disposal Authority must again consult certain persons (see above 1.5), and the

---

(1) Friends of the Earth has produced a guide to waste policy choices, 'Waste – Problem or Resource?' (15p + 7p from FOE); it includes a critique on the Government's advice on assessing the economics of recycling.

(2) An offence under s. 27 of the Control of Pollution Act, unless authorized by the local authority.

modifications must be submitted for public consultation, unless the Authority feels that no one will be prejudiced by leaving out this stage of the process. (*s 2(3) (b)*). Details of the final modification must be adequately publicised and a copy sent to the Secretary of State (*s.2 (6)(a)* and *(b)*).

When the Waste Disposal Plan has been published, you should find out if the Authority has formulated a policy for updating the Plan. Do they, for instance, envisage regular new Surveys and modifications? If you feel the initial Survey made some glaring omissions, suggest a further Survey of that area. Keep in close touch with the Authority, and, if appropriate, be prepared to campaign for changes to the Plan.

1.10 **Role of Secretary of State:** The Waste Disposal Plan does not need to be confirmed by the Secretary of State, though the Disposal Authority is obliged to send him a copy of the Plan (*s.2(6)(b)*). But the Secretary of State has the power to issue directions specifying a time by which an Authority is to perform its duties (*s.2(7)*), and, in the last resort, he may, if satisfied that an Authority has failed to perform any of the functions it should have, issue a Default Notice (*s.97 – cf 5.2*); failure to comply with directions contained in a Default Notice will result in the Secretary of State assuming the functions himself.
You may feel the Disposal Authority is failing in its obligations under Section 2. For instance, it may have failed to give proper consideration to the possibilities of reclamation (*s.4*); its arrangements for giving publicity to the Plan may not be 'adequate' (*s.2(6)(a)*); or it may appear to be making no plans for updating the Survey and Plan (*s.2(1)(d)* and *(e)*). In these circumstances, you should remind the Authority of its duties under the Act and of the Default Powers of the Department of the Environment. Where appropriate, request the DOE to issue a Default Notice (cf 5.2 below).

THE LICENCE SYSTEM   *Sections 3–11*
Commencement Order SI 1976/731
Regulations Issued SI 1976/732

1.11 *Section 2* of the Act obliges Disposal Authorities to make broad stategic plans for the disposal of waste in their area (see above 1.3–10). In contrast, *sections 3–11* introduce a detailed regulatory system for controlling the deposit of certain types of waste on land in their area. It is now an offence to tip or dump any 'controlled' waste on land, unless a LICENCE is held by the occupier of the land on which the tip is made. 'Controlled' waste is defined as 'household, industrial and commercial' waste (*s.30(1)*), and the system does not apply to, for instance, agricultural waste (which is supervised by the Ministry of Agriculture, Fisheries and Food), mining and quarrying waste (controlled by planning laws), and radioactive waste (controlled by authorizations issued by the Secretary of State for the Environment under the Radioactive Substances Act 1960)[1]. In addition the Secretary of State may issue regulations excluding types of controlled waste from the system (*s.3(1)*), and already a number of minor types of waste have been exempted.[2] These include, for instance, builder's rubble deposited on site, waste put in dustbins and skips, and waste deposited along the bank of a river during dredging operations. But waste falling within those categories which is poisonous, noxious and liable to give rise to an environmental hazard[2] (for instance, asbestos dumped in a skip) would not be exempted, and comes under the full controls of the system.

PRIVATE OPERATORS

1.12 **Applications for a Licence – Publicity:** An application for a licence to deposit controlled waste must be made to the local Disposal Authority (County Council/Greater London Council). Planning permission is also required for any new waste disposal site, and, while the Secretary of State may issue regulations for the proceeding relating to the granting of planning permission and a Disposal Licence to be held concurrently (*s.5(2)*), none have been made as yet. Planning permission must therefore be in force before the Licence is issued (*s.5(2)*); but once planning permission is granted, the Disposal Authority may not then reject outright an application for the Disposal Licence unless this is necessary to prevent pollution to water or danger to human health (*s.5(3)*). The relationship between the planning authority (normally the District Council) and the Disposal Authority is therefore crucial to the success of the new licencing system; once planning permission is granted, the Disposal Authority is severely limited in the way it can deal with the licence application. These problems are further discussed under the section dealing with conditions (see below 1.14).

Before a Disposal Licence is ever granted, it is possible to have influence on the decision. But the biggest problem is finding out in good time that an application for a Licence has been made: the Disposal Authorities have no legal duty to publicize the applications or consult members of the general public before granting applications.

As explained above, new sites will first require planning permission, and these planning applications must by law be published in the local press and displayed on site notices.[3]

(1) But note that under *s.18*, the Secretary of State may make regulations stating that agricultural, mining and quarrying waste *shall be* included as controlled waste for specified sections of the Act and in specified areas (see 1.21).
(2) Control of Pollution (Licencing of Waste Disposal) Regs. 1976/732 & Control of Pollution (Licencing of Waste Disposal) (Amendment) Regs. 1977/1185.
(3) Town & Country Planning Act 1971, *s.26* and General Development Order 1977 Article 8.

Once you have spotted a planning application which appears to relate to the disposal of controlled waste, check with your Disposal Authority when the application for the Disposal Licence is likely to be made.

Where a planning application has not been made (because, for instance, it is not a new site), or where you simply missed the publicity, you may have a problem ever finding that the application for a Disposal Licence has been made. However, some planning authorities automatically publish all planning applications in the local press (whether or not they are required to do so under the Town and Country Planning legislation), or place copies of all applications in the local public library. It is worth trying to persuade your Disposal Authority to adopt such a policy for applications for Disposal Licences.

The Disposal Authority may have decided to cut out this sort of publicity on the grounds of cost, but it may still be willing to send copies of licence applications to local amenity groups for comment. The Department of the Environment Circular on the subject (DOE 55/76) simply says, 'Waste Disposal Authorities may often wish to go beyond their statutory obligations[2] in seeking the views of other bodies.' Planning applications are often sent automatically to local organizations, and, if your group has a strong reputation in the area, it is well worthwhile requesting the Disposal Authority to be put on a consultation list; such a request could be made through a friendly councillor or officer.

If you are not making much progress with the Disposal Authority, remember that the Disposal Authority is legally obliged to consult with the local District/London Boroughs on applications.[1]

You may have better success in persuading your District or London Borough Council to keep you informed about any applications. Summing up, there is not at present a consistent policy among Disposal Authorities on publicity and consultation; this is well illustrated by some of the answers sent last year by Authorities to local Friends of the Earth groups:

> "The Council does not advertise applications but does keep them on a file which is open for inspection. Copies are available to members of the public at a charge of £1.50 each."

> "It is considered that where matters of major local importance are at issue, publicity will be given as necessary."

---

(1) The Disposal Authority must consult with local District/London Borough Councils, and the Local Water Authority – see below 1.13.

16

"The Authority does not publish applications but a description of them is taken to Public Protection Committee meetings to which the public are admitted."

"All present consultees (10) have a statutory, professional, or official local or specific involvement related to the sites as opposed to your general request."

"The Authority will not be advertising applications for waste disposal licences. . . . The Authority will not be consulting your group about licence applications because of the additional work, expense and delay involved."

1.13 **Dealing with applications:** On receipt of an Application, the Disposal Authority has a statutory duty to consult with the local Water Authority and the District/London Borough Councils ('Collection Authorities'), and any other body prescribed in regulations by the Secretary of State for the Environment, (*s.5(4)*). Under present regulations, these include the Health and Safety Executive (see below 4.3) and, in certain cases, the Institute for Geological Sciences.[1] Aside from that, the Disposal Authority has no legal duty to consider representations from other persons before making their decision.

They may refuse the application outright, but where planning permission has already been granted for the site (and this will be true in the vast majority of cases), they may only make a refusal if this would be 'necessary for the purpose of preventing pollution to water or danger to public health.' (*s.5(3)*).

If your group intends to influence a decision on a licence application, remember that even if you get to hear of the application (see above 1.12), the Disposal Authority has no legal duty to consider your representations. You must try to establish friendly relations with the Waste Disposal Officers, or produce such a compelling case, backed by an appropriate public campaign, that they have to listen to you. You may also have success working through your local district or London Borough council, since they have to be consulted by the Disposal Authority on each application, and on an especially controversial application, they may feel that the Disposal Authority is out of touch with local feelings on the issue.

If you are trying to persuade the Disposal Authority to reject the application outright (rather than impose certain conditions), you will only succeed if you can convince the Authority that the operation of the site will pollute water or be a danger to public health. This may be

(1) Control of Pollution (Licencing of Waste Disposal) Regulations (S.1. 1976/732), (s.6).

17

WASTE DISCHARGES ON LAND

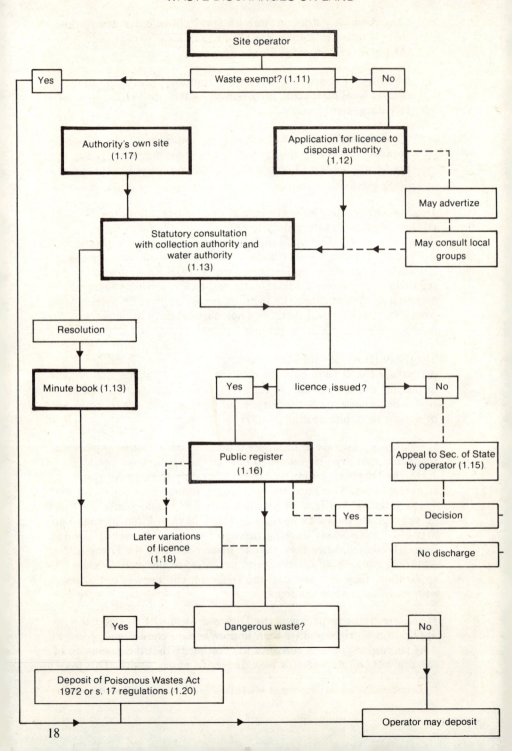

difficult in many cases, and the appropriate time to question, say, the need or siting of the proposal, will be when the planning application is considered. Planning applications for the site will be advertised and copies available for public inspection in the planning register of your District or London Borough Council. The District Council may consider the application themselves, but they may decide to pass on applications relating to waste disposal sites to the County Council on the grounds that they are a 'county matter'. This will depend on local administrative arrangements, but you should find out from the District Council whether they have made any policy decision on the matter.

Once you hear of any proposals for a waste disposal site, keep in touch with the planning officers of your District Council for news of the progress of the planning application. There will be certain time-limits for making representations, and it is important to keep within these.[1]

1.14 **Conditions attached to Licences:** Although the Disposal Authority's power to reject outright a licence application is limited by *s.5(3)* of the Act (see above 1.12), it may impose such conditions on the licence as it sees fit. *(s.6(2))*. The Act lists a number of areas to which conditions may relate, and these include the duration of the licence, the kinds and qualities of waste which may be treated, precautions to be taken on the site, and the hours of working *(s.6(2))*. But the list is not exhaustive, (it is stated to be 'without prejudice' to the Authority's general power to impose conditions), and, although the Secretary of State for the Environment has the power to issue regulations specifying the conditions which may or may not be imposed by the Authority *(s.6(1))*, he has indicated that he does not, as yet, intend to exercise this power.[2] A Disposal Authority therefore has considerable discretion in the way they handle a licence application at present.

Before the Control of Pollution Act came into force, waste disposal sites were controlled solely by conditions attached to planning permissions, but, with the arrival of the new system, local authorities have now been advised that 'conditions attached to new planning permissions should not therefore extend to matters which are more appropriate to the disposal licensing system.'[3] Planning conditions should relate to the use and appearance of the land (access, tree-planting, landscaping and eventual restoration), while conditions of the

---

(1) *Polluters Pay* does not deal with methods of opposing planning applications – for information on this subject, see, for instance, "New Citizens Guide to Town and Country Planning" (Town and Country Planning Association).

(2) DOE Circular 55/76, para. 31.

(3) ibid, para. 43.

Disposal licence will deal with the day-to-day operations of the site, and the protection of public health and the environment. But there may well be problems in the operation of the joint system. Disposal licence conditions may last only as long as the licence, and this ceases at the end of disposal operations; such conditions cannot therefore relate to areas such as continued maintenance of bore-holes, or leachate treatment systems. These matters would have to be included in conditions attached to the original planning permission (which can continue after the end of operations), but the planning officers or committee may not be technically competent to deal with these types of problems. Furthermore, some conditions, such as the working hours of the site, could be said to be appropriate planning *or* disposal licence matters; there is a clear danger that they will not be fully considered because each authority or committee thinks the other is dealing with these matters. All the advice the Department of the Environment has been able to offer is that, 'in these circumstances, it seems right that there may sometimes be an area of overlap and that authorities must resolve this problem when it arises.'[1] Finally, not only will different officers and committees deal with the planning and disposal licence applications, but it may well be different authorities; this depends on whether the District Council decides to refer the planning application up to County level, as being a 'county matter'. There is no provision, at present, that a planning authority, in dealing with an application relating to a waste disposal site, must first consult with the Disposal Authority, and this again may provide a source of communication problems.

The Disposal Authorities have been given a very wide discretion as to the type of conditions they may impose on a Disposal Licence, but, since the law is new, Authorities will be feeling their way for the first years. Local Groups may therefore be able to exercise considerable influence on the conditions attached to a licence, but you should be fully aware of the possible problems of the relationship between the planning and the disposal licencing systems. Before suggesting conditions, it is worthwhile studying Waste Management Paper No. 4 (HMSO 1976), which advises local authorities on the matters to be taken into account in the formulation of licence conditions.

If you find that neither the planning authority nor the disposal authority are dealing satisfactorily with matters such as the erection of protective fencing round the tip, the working hours of the site, or the restoration of the site after operations have ceased, you should inform the Department of the Environment. They could solve the problem by issuing regulations under *s.6(1)* specifying certain conditions which must be attached to Disposal Licences, or by using their powers under *s.5(2)* to specify that the proceedings relating to the planning and licence applications should be conducted at the same time.

(1) Waste Management Paper No. 4, para. 4.9 (HMSO 1976)

1.15 **Appeal to Secretary of State:** If the Disposal Authority refuses an application, or grants it subject to unreasonable conditions, the applicant may appeal to the Secretary of State for the Environment (in Wales, the Secretary of State for Wales) *(s.10)*. Before reaching a decision, the Secretary of State may hold a public inquiry.

The Authority is deemed to have refused the application if they make no decision for 2 months from the date of receiving the application, or such longer period as they may agree with the applicant *(s.6(5))*.

On a particularly controversial case, a local inquiry may be the only forum at which the facts will come out into the open, or where your case will be fully heard. But the Secretary of State for the Environment has no power to 'call-in' a disposal licence application and initiate a public inquiry, as he has with a planning application[1]; if you want a public inquiry, you will have to persuade the Disposal Authority to refuse the application and thereby set in motion the appeal procedure. But their grounds for refusing a licence application are very limited (see above 1.13), and you should always try to force a public inquiry at the initial planning application stage, if you are likely to be successful.

Recently a planning inquiry into a local authority's proposed waste disposal site in North Wales demonstrated the value of mounting opposition at this planning stage rather than later. The Secretary of State decided against the local authority on the grounds that pollution would be caused by the operation of the site.

The Department of the Environment have suggested that in certain circumstances, a planning inquiry and a disposal licence inquiry should be held jointly[2], and you should lobby for this if you are concerned about the overlap problems outlined above (1.14).

1.16 **The Public Register:** Disposal Authorities are required to maintain a Public Register, containing certain particulars of Disposal Licences issued by them, and copies of entries must be available to members of the public at reasonable charges *(s.6(4))*. The minimum information that must be contained in entries has been specified in regulations made by the Secretary of State[3], and includes the 'form of deposit or disposal', the 'types of waste', and 'any conditions attached to the licence'. Disposal Authorities have a discretion how much further information to put in the Public Register, but they have been advised

---

(1) Town & Country Planning Act 1971, s.35.

(2) DOE Circular, 55/76, para. 37.

(3) Control of Pollution (Licencing of Waste Disposal) Regulations 1976 (1976/732), section 5.

by the Department of the Environment that, unless trade secrets are involved, the register might 'most conveniently consist of filed copies of current licences.'[1]

If you intend to become involved in the subject of waste disposal, it is important to find out first where the Public Register of site licences is kept, the times of opening and the charge for copying entries. By studying the register you should be able to discover the categories and quantities of controlled waste being deposited in your area, and the conditions under which this is supposed to be taking place. You should find out from the Disposal Authority whether they intend to follow the advice of the Department of the Environment to enter copies of existing licences in the Public Register.

1.17 *DISPOSAL AUTHORITIES' OWN SITES* Disposal Authorities sometimes operate their own disposal sites, and special arrangements will then apply. A Disposal Licence is not required (*s.11(1)*), but before operating a site, the Disposal Authority must pass a formal resolution, stating the conditions under which they will operate their own site. (*s.11(2)(c)*). The resolution will be contained in the minute book of the County Council, or appropriate Committee (which are open to public inspection), but the particulars of the resolution must also be filed in the Public Register of Disposal Licences (*s.11 (10)*). Before passing the resolution, the Disposal Authority must consult with the Water Authority and local District or London Borough Councils (*s.11(3)*).

The Authority may operate its own site only under conditions designed to prevent water pollution, a danger to public health, and a 'serious detriment to the amenities of the locality' (*s.11(2)*).

You will have problems in finding out that your Disposal Authority intends to operate its own site since there are no publicity provisions written into the Act (see above 1.12), and, even if you do, the Authority is under no legal duty to consider your representations. If you want to have influence, you may have to mount a strong campaign, or keep in close contact with a friendly councillor or officer – and there are times when the two approaches will not be mutually exclusive! It will also be sensible to lobby your District Council, who must be consulted before the resolution is passed. In particular, make sure that appropriate conditions are included in the resolution.

1.18 **Subsequent Variation or Revocation of Licences:** Where it appears to the Disposal Authority that the operation of a site is causing water pollution,[2] a danger to public health or a serious detriment to the local

---

(1) DOE Circular 55/76, para 38.

(2) See below 2.9.

amenities, it *must* either revoke the licence or vary the conditions attached to it (*s. 7(1)(b) and 7(4)*). The licence holder may appeal to the Secretary of State, who may hold a public inquiry; compensation will be payable if the Secretary of State holds that the Disposal Authority acted unreasonably (*s.10(3)(b)*). The Disposal Authority also has a discretion to vary licence conditions to the extent they feel desirable, provided that this is not likely to cause unreasonable expenditure to the licence holder (*s.7(1)*).

Similar principles apply to the Disposal Authority's own sites. Where, in the opinion of the Authority, the operation of its site is causing water pollution, danger to the public health, or a serious detriment to the local amenities (*s.11(2) and (8)*).

If you feel the conditions under which tipping is taking place gives cause for concern, organize a campaign to persuade the Disposal Authority to revoke the licence or modify its conditions (or, in the case of its own sites, pass an appropriate resolution). This might happen if you were to discover, say, material being tipped where the site is unfenced and children use nearby land as a playground. Notice the conditions under which the Authority must act, though you should remember that circumstances that appear to you to be causing water pollution etc. may not appear so to the Disposal Authority. It is unlikely that, except in extreme cases, an Authority will take such drastic action, because of the possibility of paying compensation. But in cases where a modification of the conditions will solve the problem, a Disposal Authority, especially if backed by strong public pressure, should be able to persuade an operator that the extra expense in complying with stricter conditions is not 'unreasonable', according to *s.7(1).*

1.19 **Enforcement:** It is a criminal offence to deposit controlled waste on any land unless a disposal licence is in force, and the conditions, if any, are followed (*s.3(1) and (2)*). In addition, there are particularly severe penalties where such waste is shown to be poisonous, noxious or polluting, *and* the dumping is likely to give rise to an 'environmental hazard' (*s.3(3)*). An 'environmental hazard' occurs where the dumping of waste subjects 'persons or animals to a material risk of death, injury or impairment of health', or threatens any public water supply (*s.4(5)*).

Disposal Authorities are under a statutory duty to ensure that licence conditions are followed, and to take steps to ensure that the operation of the site does not cause water pollution, a danger to public health, or a serious detriment to the local amenities (*s.9(1)*). In cases of emergency, authorized officers of the Authority may enter the site to carry out necessary remedial action, and recover the cost from the licence holder (*s.9(2) & (3)*).

In the present climate of public expenditure, many Disposal Authorities may find themselves unable to perform all their statutory duties of enforcement. Once licences are issued, it is uncertain how much will be done to monitor the sites to ensure compliance with conditions, and Disposal Authorities may be unaware of unlicenced tipping in their area. In these circumstances, campaign objectives are more likely to be achieved by initial cooperation with the Disposal Authority rather than confrontation, and local groups could offer Authorities a helping hand as watchdogs.[1] Smaller Authorities, and District or London Borough Councils may even welcome the expertise a group has to offer.

Where the dumping of waste is a problem, check that the waste is 'controlled' (see above 1.11), and, if it is, that it is not permitted waste under the Regulations (see above 1.11)[2]. If the waste is not permitted, there should be a licence issued, and this will be revealed in the Public Register (above 1.16). If no licence has been issued, report the fact at once to the Disposal Authority. Where there is a licence, check the conditions, and if these are not being followed, again report the matter to the Disposal Authority.

Make sure the Authority takes satisfactory action to deal with the problem. If necessary, you may have to start a public campaign, and in the last resort, there is nothing to stop you, as an individual initiating criminal proceedings yourself in the local Magistrates Court. Clearly, you should only consider such a course, if the Authority persists in doing nothing about the problem, and you are absolutely sure of your facts.[3]

1.20 **Special Controls for Dangerous Wastes**

Section 17
Commencement Order SI 1975/2118
Regulations Issued: likely by end 1979

Under *section 17,* the Secretary of State for the Environment may issue regulations concerning the handling and disposal of particularly dangerous wastes. These controls would be in addition to the licencing system, and could relate, for instance, to the storage and carriage of such wastes, and the keeping of records.

---

(1) Campaigns in this area have achieved some notable successes. The Deposit of Poisonous Waste Act 1972 was passed as a result of the vigorous campaigning of a local amenity group in the Midlands who discovered the dangerous practice of dumping drums of cyanide.

(2) Remember that any waste that can be said to be noxious, polluting or environmentally hazardous will fall outside the Regulations (see above 1.11).

(3) At this point, it would be wise to seek legal advice

No regulations have yet been made under this section, and toxic wastes are still controlled by the Deposit of Poisonous Waste Act 1972, which requires three days notice to be given to both the Disposal and the Water Authorities before the disposal of certain wastes is made.

1.21 Wastes other than 'Controlled'

Section 18
Commencement Order SI 1976/731
Regulations Issued NOT YET

The licencing system applies only to 'controlled waste', covering household, industrial and commercial waste (see above 1.11). But under section 18, the Secretary of State for the Environment has the power to issue regulations stating that specified provisions of the Act shall apply to either agricultural or mining and quarrying wastes. The regulations may limit the application of the Act to particular areas. Before issuing such regulations (and none have been made as yet), the Secretary of State must consult 'such bodies as he considers appropriate'.

Where the deposit of uncontrolled waste is causing a persistent problem in your area, campaign for the Department of the Environment to issue regulations under this section. Such a campaign is likely to be long and difficult but worth pursuing if you have discovered a major gap in the existing controls.

Under *s.18(2)*, it is a criminal offence to deposit uncontrolled waste which is poisonous, noxious or polluting *and* which is likely to give rise to an 'environmental hazard' (see above 1.19), unless this was authorized under any other enactment; planning permission under the Town and Country Planning Acts is not sufficient authorization.

Where the deposit of waste other than 'controlled' is causing a problem, you must first find out whether the dumping of the waste was authorized under another statute (such as the Radioactive Substances Act 1960). The owner of the site may inform you, but it may involve considerable research around different Government or local Authority departments. Existing planning permission is not sufficient authorization, and where there appears to be no satisfactory authorization, and the waste can be described as polluting, noxious or poisonous, and likely to give rise to an environmental hazard, a criminal offence may have been committed. Report the matter at once to the Disposal Authority, or the police. The Disposal Authority may be slow to act since the waste is not 'controlled', and in the last resort you may have to initiate, or threaten to initiate criminal proceedings yourself.[1]

(1) but see comments above 1.19.

1.22 **LITTER PLANS**   *Section 24*
Commencement Order NOT YET
Regulations Not Required

Under this section, all local authorities in each County (including
Parish Councils and National Park Authorities) have a duty to consult
with each other from time to time and 'with such voluntary bodies as
the authorities consider appropriate' about the steps they are to take to
abate litter in the County. In addition, the County Council must
prepare, and from time to time revise, a Statement of their plans. This
'Litter Abatement Statement' must be a publicized and a copy made
available for public inspection at the Councils' principal office.

**You may consider litter to be a side issue which merely reflects
inappropriate or excessive use of packaging, but it is probably
worthwhile playing a part in the preparation of the litter plan for your
County. You should find out with which voluntary bodies the
Authorities intend to consult and persuade them that your group
should be included; if your group is not formally included in the
consultation process, you should still try to convince your District or
Parish Councils of your ideas. Clearly the litter plan will not be such a
basic strategic document as the Waste Disposal Plan (see above
1.3–10), but an idea that might be included in the plan is a publicity
campaign by the authorities on the excessive use of packaging, and its
consequences to pollution and resources. Other issues that could be
discussed are the use of planning laws to control the spread of take-
away food shops causing a major litter problem, or the curbing of
excessive leafletting by the Councils themselves. You should study the
Litter Abatement Statement when it is published, and suggest areas
where it could be revised, especially if it does not support principles
contained in the Waste Disposal Plan (see above 1.3–10).**

1.23 **RECLAMATION OF WASTE and
PRODUCTION OF HEAT AND** *Sections 20/21*
ELECTRICITY FROM WASTE Commencement Order 1975/21
No regulations required

Section 20 gives Disposal Authorities wide-ranging powers to
undertake recycling and reclamation schemes for waste either belonging
to them (i.e. after it has been delivered to them by the District or
London Borough Councils) or to other persons who ask them to deal
with their waste under this section.

Section 21 gives Disposal Authorities power to use waste to produce
heat for their own premises, or to sell the heat, subject to making an
annual report to the Secretary of State for the Environment. They may
also produce electricity from waste, but where they wish to sell the

electricity or to use it other than in the installation where it was produced, they must consult the Central Electricity Generating Board and receive the approval of the Secretary of State.

Sections 20 and 21 are discretionary powers, and given the present shortage of finance, local authorities are unlikely to be interested in schemes requiring large expenditure. Local groups could capitalize on this situation by offering cooperation and expertise, and the Authorities should be reminded that s.20 gives them explicit powers to establish a commercial recycling business. Several authorities have been running experimental paper recycling schemes in recent years, and this new legislation gives you an excuse to apply further pressure to encourage them to set up new schemes or make the existing ones permanent. Public response to such schemes is generally excellent – you should persuade the Authority that the public would welcome recycling centres, and even offer help with publicity.

1.24 **Crown buildings:** Part I of the Act does not apply to Crown buildings, but the Department of the Environment has requested Government Departments to comply with the spirit of the Act, and to ensure that local Disposal Authorities approve their operating standards.

PART II: WATER

INTRODUCTION

2.1 *Part II* of the Control of Pollution Act is concerned mainly with rivers, estuaries and other water courses, and it replaces most of the existing and highly complicated laws on water pollution. The Act strengthens the present system of controls, which is based on the granting of Consents by Regional Water Authorities (see below 2.3). In granting these consents, the Water Authorities have a wide discretion as to the effluents and level of discharge they will allow in each case. For some time, the E.E.C. Commission in Brussels has been pressing for uniform discharge levels to be laid down in law, but this principle is not likely to be accepted in this country. Instead, it is proposed to establish non-statutory quality objectives for individual rivers, and Consents will be issued in the light of these objectives.

The main effect of this part of the Control of Pollution Act will be to provide new rights of public access to information, and despite the complicated nature of the law, the Act should provide useful and important opportunities for campaigns. The latest River Pollution Survey in England and Wales revealed that about half of the industrial discharges failed to meet prescribed standards, though the number of criminal proceedings initiated was minimal. With the new rights of access to information, individuals will be able to study for themselves the local situation, put pressure on the Water Authorities, or even initiate their own legal proceedings to ensure adherence to the water standards in their area. But one word of warning — the subject of water pollution will often call for considerable scientific expertise, especially in interpreting data, and any group would be well advised to seek the advize of someone with experience in this area, if they are to make real progress.

2.2 **Commencement dates:** Most of the Sections in Part II are NOT YET in force, though the Government has recently announced that it intends to bring the main provisions of this Part into full operation by the end of 1979.[1] Until this happens, control of water pollution will continue to be by a system of Consents similar to that described below, but without the provisions relating to public access to information, and the right of private prosecution. This system is administered by the Water Authorities under the Rivers (Prevention of Pollution) Acts 1951 and 1961.

ADMINISTRATIVE ARRANGEMENTS

2.3 **Water Authorities:** The system of controls is operated by ten Water Authorities covering England and Wales, and established by the Water

---

(1) D.O.E. Press Notice 199, April 13th 1978

Act 1973. They are corporate bodies, whose members are appointed by the Secretary of State for the Environment.

Water Authorities are probably less susceptible than elected local authorities to public pressure. Each Authority, however, includes members from the Local Authority in their area, and a group, making no headway with the Authority itself, might have better success in directing their efforts at their local representatives on the Authority. A local Water Authority will be found under 'Water' in the telephone book, and the list of members of the Authority can be obtained from the Authority itself, or their Annual Reports of the Authority, found in most public libraries.

2.4 **Scope of controls:** The Act controls two main sources of water pollution: discharges of *Poisonous matter/Solid waste (s.31*: 2.7-2.11), and *Trade and Sewage effluent (s.32*: 2.12.) Unless the Water Authority has granted a Consent (2.13-2.20), any such discharge would normally be a criminal offence.[1]

The system is made particularly complicated because not all areas of water are covered in each section of the Act. A number of different terms such as 'restricted' and 'relevant' waters are used in the legislation; these all receive detailed definitions in later sections of the Act.[2]

The system of controls under *Part II* do NOT apply to certain important areas such as Sewers, Canals or the Sea outside the 3 mile limit.

SEWERS are vested in the Water Authorities, and they control the discharge of trade effluents into each sewer by a system of Consents issued under the Public Health (Drainage of Trade Premises) Act 1937 and the Public Health Act 1961, recently strengthened by *ss. 43-5* of the Control of Pollution Act. This is an area of growing importance since Water Authorities often encourage industries to discharge their effluent into the sewers rather than into rivers. But while general information about the quality of sewage effluent will be found in the Authorities' Annual Reports (available in most public libraries or from the Authorities) the Public Health legislation does not provide for the publication of applications for Consents or of the details of Consents and Samples. The eventual discharge of the sewage by Water Authorities into rivers or the Sea is governed by the Control of Pollution Act under *s. 32* (see 2.12 below); the provisions of the Act apply to the Authorities as much as anyone else.[3]

---

(1) each section also provides several other, less important, defences—details below.
(2) the definitions are mostly listed in S.56 of the Act.
(3) See below 2(5).

CANALS are generally vested in the British Waterways Board, and discharges are made into them under individual contracts.

The SEA: other legislation covers pollution of the Sea, though *s.32* of the Control of Pollution Act (see below 2.12), which governs trade or sewage effluent, applies to pipes which end outside the 3 mile limit.

2.5 **Water Authorities' own discharges:** Generally the provisions of the Act apply to Water Authorities who are responsible for discharges from all sewage works.

2.6 **Crown Property:** the controls do not apply to Government Departments, though they will to public corporations such as the National Coal Board.

ENTRIES OF POISONOUS MATTER

Section 31

Commencement Order   Not Yet (likely late 1979)

Regulations Issued   Not Yet (likely la 1979)

2.7 Under *s.31(i)(c)*, a person is guilty of an offence if he causes, or permits any poisonous, noxious, or polluting matter to enter into any 'relevant waters'. The term 'relevant waters' includes (i) rivers, inland waters (natural or artificial), but lakes or ponds which do not discharge into a river are not included unless they have been specifically named by the Secretary of State in regulations *(s. 56(3))* (all the waters in (i) are known in the Act, rather misleadingly, as 'streams') (ii) estuaries round the coast and the sea within 3 miles (known as 'controlled waters') (iii) underground waters specified by the Water Authority.

The terms 'poisonous, noxious or polluting', which were used in the previous legislation, have never been interpreted by the Courts. Presumably, they would cover matter harmful to the environment in general, as well as that harmful to humans only.

Under *s.31(i)(c)*, a person will be guilty of an offence if he allows solid waste matter, whether 'poisonous' or not, to enter any stream (defined in (i) above), or tidal waters.

Where you are concerned about pollution in a particular stretch of water, find out whether it comes under the control of a Water Authority and these sections of the Act. Where, say, pollution of a land-locked lake or pond (which would generally fall outside the definition of 'streams' here) is causing particular concern, and existing controls are

not coping adequately[1], campaign for the Secretary of State to issue regulations under *s.56(3)* of the Act, bringing the particular lake or pond under the control of the Water Authority.

2.8   *s.31* provides a blanket offence, but it lists a number of important defences to any proceedings. The most important is that the entry was authorized by a CONSENT issued by the Water Authority *(s.31(2)(a)),* and the system of Consent is dealt with in detail below. (see 2.13).

The other defences are that
  (i)   the entry was authorized by a DISPOSAL LICENCE granted under Part I of the Act *(31(2)(a))*
  (ii) the entry was in accordance with Good Agricultural Practice *(s.31(2)(c))*
  (iii) the entry was caused by an emergency *(s.31(2)(a))*

Each of these defences is explained below.

Where you suspect that waters are being polluted by acts outlined in 2.7, first make sure that one of the defences above does not apply. If none do, a criminal offence may have been committed, and you should inform the Water Authority. Where the activity does seem to be covered by one of the defences, you may still have the basis for a campaign.

2.9   **Defence (i)** Entry Authorized by a Disposal Licence *(s.31(2)(a))*
The disposal of certain types of waste on land requires a licence issued by the County or Greater London Council, (see Part I). Before issuing a Disposal Licence, the Council must consult the local Water Authority *(s.5(4)),* and if the bodies disagree over the issue of the licence or the conditions to be attached to a licence, they may refer the matter to the Secretary of State for decision. A Council **must** reject a licence application where it is satisfied that this is necessary for the purpose of preventing water pollution *(s.5(3)).* But once the licence has been granted, it will not, then be an offence under *s.31* to discharge polluting matter into waters, provided this was authorized or was in consequence of an act authorized by the licence; this would presumably cover a situation where the Authorities had not foreseen the water pollution that could be caused by the granting of a licence.

Where you suspect that an activity which will require a Disposal Licence may cause water pollution make sure both the Water Authority and the Council are fully aware of your case before the licence is granted. Better still, object on this ground when planning

(1) for instance, District or London Borough Councils have powers under the Public Health Act 1936 to deal with ponds and watercourses so foul as to be prejudicial to public health.

permission for the activity is first sought, as you will probably stand a greater chance of success at this stage (see Part I, 1.12 etc.)

Where a disposal licence is already in force, the Council has a duty to revoke the licence, or vary the conditions attached to it, if this is necessary to prevent the pollution of water. *(s.7(1)(b) and (4))*. Once the Licence is revoked, it will become an offence to continue the activities, unless any of the other defences in *s.31* are applicable. The Council must also take any other steps necessary to ensure that water pollution is not caused by an activity authorized by a Disposal Licence, and, in an emergency, the Authority may enter the licencee's land, carry out any necessary work and charge the cost to the licencee *(s.9(1)(2) and (3))*

Where the pollution has already taken place and is covered by a Disposal Licence, make sure that the Council prevents further pollution by either revoking or modifying the Licence. Where there appears to be an emergency — and the licencee is taking no steps to prevent the pollution — persuade the Council to carry out the remedial work themselves under *s.9*.

2.10 **Defence (ii)** Entry attributable to an act or omision which is in accordance Good Agricultural Practice *(s.31(2)(c))*.

'Good Agricultural Practice' is defined in the Act as any practice recommended in a code approved by the Ministry of Agriculture, Fisheries and Food *(s.31(9))*, and these Codes should be available from the Ministry. But where the Water Authority feel that certain acts or omissions, which would normally be good agricultural practice, have caused or are likely to cause water pollution, they may request the Secretary of State for the Environment to ban these practices in certain areas. The procedure is described in *section 51*. Copies of the Authority's application must be sent to the Ministry of Agriculture, Fisheries and Food and to the occupier of the affected land. The occupier may within 28 days make representations to the Secretary of State, after which the Secretary of State may then issue a formal Notice requesting the occupier to desist from the activities specified. He may issue a Notice less restrictive than that requested by the Water Authority *(s.51(3)(a))*, and he may at any time cancel the Notice. Details of the Notice, or of cancellations, must be entered on the Water Register, and available for public inspection. (see below 2.21). Failure to comply with the Notice is not an offence in itself, but once it has been served the defence of 'good agricultural practice' will no longer be available to proceedings under *section 31*.

Where you find that entries of polluting matter into waters have been made in accordance with the MAFF Codes of good agricultural

practice, you must persuade the Water Authority to request the Department of the Environment to serve a Notice under *s.51*. This is likely to be successful only where normal farming practices are causing pollution because of special local reasons. In considering whether or not to issue a Notice, the Secretary of State for the Environment is obliged to consider only the farmer's representations, but if you find out that the Authority has made a request (and they are not obliged to tell you), you should send your arguments to the D.O.E., and copies to the Ministry of Agriculture, Fisheries and Food, since they are likely to be consulted. You are more likely to be persuasive if you can show that the farmer could, without much difficulty, adopt some other practice which would be less likely to cause pollution. Also remember that the discharge of liquid effluents into waters from farms will require a Consent under *s.32* (see below 2.12), whether or not this is in accordance with good agricultural practice.

2.11 **Defence (iii)** — Entry caused because of an emergency.

There will be no defence under *s.31* if the entry was caused because of an emergency in order to avoid danger to the public. As soon as possible, full details of the entry must be sent to the Water Authority.

ENTRIES OF TRADE EFFLUENT	*Section 32*
	Commencement Order Not Yet (likely late 1979)
	Regulations Issued Not Yet (likely late 1979)

2.12 Under *Section 32* it is an offence to discharge trade or sewage effluent into all 'relevant' waters (see 2.7), inland lakes or ponds unconnected with a stream; onto land; or from a pipe into the sea. *(s.32(1)(a))*. Trade effluent includes any liquid discharged from premises used for trade or industry, including agriculture. *(s.105(1))*. There are only two defences – (i) the discharge was caused by an emergency (see above 2.10) or (ii) was permitted by a Consent issued by the Water Authority (see below 2.13 and following).

THE CONSENT SYSTEM	*Sections 34-40*
	Commencement Order Not Yet (likely late 1979)
	Regulations Issued Not Yet (likely late 1979)

2.13 No offences will be committed under *sections 31* and *32,* provided a Consent has been issued by the Water Authority and its conditions observed. The following sections therefore provide the basic structure of the system of pollution control, and since they provide most of the opportunities for public participation, they are of importance to anyone campaigning in this area.

Methods of influencing Water Authorities in the granting of NEW CONSENTS are explained in 2.14–2.20; the problems of EXISTING CONSENTS are dealt with in 2.28–2.35.

2.14 **NEW CONSENTS:** Applications for a consent to discharge effluent or other matter into waters are made to the Water Authority, who may grant the consent, subject to any reasonable conditions *(s.34(1) and (2))*. Such conditions would have to relate to the prevention of water pollution (rather than, say, relating to noise or other amenity considerations), and would cover such matters as the quality, quantity and timing of discharges, and the keeping of records. Once the Consent has been granted, this will provide a good defence to any proceedings under *sections 31* (above, 2.7) and *32* (above, 2.12)[1].

2.15 Applications for Consents must be placed in the Water Register, open to public inspection (see below 2.21), and with two important exceptions, they must be publicized in the London Gazette and in the local press for two consecutive weeks. The Authority must consider all representations made to them concerning the Application within 6 weeks *(s.36(1))*[2]

2.16 **No publicity for Applications:** Publicity will not occur where either (i) the Water Authority considers that the proposed discharge will have no appreciable effect *(s.36(4))*; applications would still be placed in the Register
or (ii) The Secretary of State for the Environment has granted an Exemption Certificate to the applicant on the grounds that publicity would either be contrary to the public interest **or** would prejudice to an unreasonable degree some private interest by disclosing information about a trade secret *(s.42)*; the application will not be placed in the Register, though the Exemption Certificate must be placed there. (see below: 2.26).

Where you intend to affect ⁺he granting of Consents, you must keep a close watch for the publication of Applications in the legal ɔections of the local press, or, better still, regularly inspect the Water Register. Water Authorities may decide to send automatically all copies of

---

(1) But owners of land adjoining rivers (known in law as 'riparian owners') may still in certain circumstances bring private proceedings against polluters under the old common law of nuisance; see further 2.32.

(2) the 6 weeks period begins from the date of publication in the London Gazette, which must not be earlier than the first publication in the local press; the notice should give the final date by which representations may be made.

applications to local amenity groups with a good reputation, in much the same way as some groups receive lists of planning applications from local authorities; it is worth at least requesting the Water Authority to do so. In addition, local authorities (either District or County Councils, depending on local arrangements) will receive copies of applications for comment (unless an Exemption Certificate has been granted by the Department of the Environment), and a friendly councillor or officer may keep you informed of any applications. At this stage, it is uncertain to what degree Water Authorities will exercise their discretion not to publicize applications on the grounds that the discharge will have no appreciable effect. Where you find they have decided against publicity on an application (this may be difficult simply because the application is not published, but it will be entered on the Water Register), there will be little you can do to affect that decision. But if you feel they have made a wrong decision, it will be worth requesting them to justify their action, since this may persuade them to think more carefully the next time.

Where notice of an application has been published, it will almost certainly contain fairly detailed particulars of the proposed discharges, though, as yet, there are no regulations issued as to notices. You should be able to assess the impact of the proposals, though this may require the help of someone with some expertise in the subject of water pollution (a member of a local university or polytechnic, for example) and you could also ask the Water Authority itself for its own estimate of the impact of the proposed discharge.

If you decide to oppose the application, it is very important to send your representations to the Water Authority within the six week period, since this can give you certain statutory rights of appeal (see below: 2.18-20). You may feel that your own objections may not carry enough weight by themselves, and it is worthwhile persuading the local authority or parish council to oppose the Application; an approach to a councillor or officer, coupled with a story in the local press, would be the first step.

PUBLIC INQUIRIES

2.17 Public Inquiries can be a most important forum at which to make the views of a group known, and they provide an opportunity to cross-examine the applicants on the detailed implications of their proposal.

In three situations (2.18, 19 & 20) it is possible that the Secretary of State for the Environment will hold a public inquiry into an Application for a Consent.

37

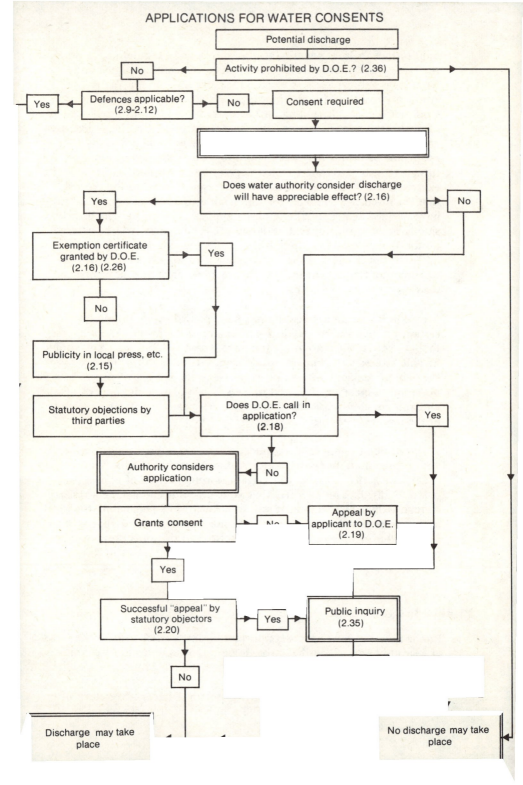

APPLICATIONS FOR WATER CONSENTS

Potential discharge

Activity prohibited by D.O.E.? (2.36)

No

Defences applicable? (2.9-2.12)

Yes

No

Consent required

Does water authority consider discharge will have appreciable effect? (2.16)

Yes

No

Exemption certificate granted by D.O.E. (2.16) (2.26)

Yes

No

Publicity in local press, etc. (2.15)

Statutory objections by third parties

Does D.O.E. call in application? (2.18)

Yes

No

Authority considers application

Grants consent

No

Appeal by applicant to D.O.E. (2.19)

Yes

Successful "appeal" by statutory objectors (2.20)

Yes

Public inquiry (2.35)

No

Discharge may take place

No discharge may take place

2.18 **'Called-in Applications'** *(s.35):* Where an Application has been made, the Secretary of State may call it in for determination by himself rather than the Water Authority, and where he has done so, he may hold a local inquiry before announcing a final decision. At present, local inquiries invariably take place where planning applications are called-in by the Secretary of State, and the practice is likely to be followed here. Persons who have made representations within the statutory six week period to the Authority will have a statutory right to appear at the Inquiry; other objectors will no doubt be heard at the discretion of the Inspector holding the Inquiry.

The Department of the Environment will probably call-in only applications involving a particularly difficult decision, or one that has more than local importance. If you feel this is the case, you should start a campaign at an early stage to persuade the Department to use its powers under *section 35.* **This will involve letters directed to the Secretary of State, press stories, petitions, and an immense amount of time and effort.**

2.19 **Appeals against Refusals** *(s.39):* Where a Water Authority has refused to grant a consent, or granted it subject to unreasonable conditions, the Applicant may appeal to the Secretary of State. *(s.39(1)).* Before making a decision, the Secretary of State must consider any further written representations from those people who originally sent in written objections to the Authority within the statutory six week period *(39(5))* (see above 2.15). In addition, the Secretary of State has a discretion to hold a local public inquiry before announcing his decision *(s.96).* Details of the appeal procedure will be laid down in regulations.

Appeals against the refusal of planning permission are by far the most common source of local planning inquiries, and the same will probably be true in the case of Applications for water Consents. Again, it is important to have made the initial written objections to the Water Authority within the statutory six weeks period, since this gives you a right of making further representations to the Department of the Environment, and will give you a statutory right to appear at the public inquiry, if it is held.

In most cases, achieving a call-in by the Department of the Environment under *section 35* (2.18) will be difficult, given that the Department will generally be loath to interfere with the autonomy of a Water Authority. If you want a local inquiry, your best route may lie in persuading the Water Authority to refuse the Consent, since, on appeal by the applicant, there will always be a public inquiry before the Department of the Environment makes a decision. In a controversial case, the Authority may be quite willing to take this course which in effect allows them to pass the buck to the Government.

2.20 **'Appeals' by statutory objectors** *(s.36(6)):* When the Water Authority proposes to grant a Consent, it must first inform all those who made representations within the statutory six week period (see above: 2.15). These objectors then have three weeks in which to request the Secretary of State to 'call-in' the application under *section 35,* and the Authority may not grant the Consent within that period. *(s.36(6)(b) and (c)).* An objector making such a request must inform the Authority that he has done so, and the Authority must then delay any decision until the Secretary of State gives permission *(s.36(6)(c)).*

This section gives statutory objectors a second chance to achieve a call-in by the Department of the Environment, and, in effect, is a right of appeal against the Authority's proposed decision. This right is not found in planning legislation, and it remains to be seen just how effective it will prove to be. Clearly, if you have already failed to persuade the Department of the Environment to call-in the application, and the Water Authority is proposing to grant the Consent, you are probably on a losing case anyway. But you may be successful if you can show convincing new reasons for a public inquiry (this could be increased public concern or evidence which has only just come to light), and an appeal under this section, coupled with a concerted campaign for a public inquiry, could have the desired effect.

THE PUBLIC REGISTER   *Section 41*

Commencement Order   Not Yet
(likely late 1979)
Regulations Issued   Not Yet
(likely late 1979)

2.21 Under *section 41,* each Water Authority must maintain a Public Register containing the following information:
  (i)   Applications for Consents.
  (ii) Details of Consents Granted.
  (iii) Details of Samples of effluent and water taken by the Water Authority, together with details of steps to be taken by the Authority as a result of information obtained from these samples.
  (iv) Notices issued under *S.51* requesting an occupier to desist from an activity which would normally be a good agricultural practice (see 2.10).
  (v)   Certificates granted by the Secretary of State giving exemption from publicity (see 2.16).

The Register must be open for public inspection at all reasonable hours, and facilities are to be provided to allow the public copies of entries, on payment of reasonable charges. *(s.41(2)(b)).*

The Water Register represents an important source of information to the public, and should be fully used. Under previous legislation, the register of Consents was open only 'to persons appearing to the Authority to be interested in the outlet' from which the effluent flowed, and this had generally been interpreted to mean only persons who owned land next to the water into which the discharges were made. Now anyone has a right to examine the Register, and the change in the law is the result of a long debate between industry and those who have been concerned to have the full facts on water pollution out in the open. In its Second Report, the Royal Commission on Environmental Pollution stated that, 'the waters into which the pollutants are discharged are public property: interest in the nature and quality of these pollutants is entirely justified.' The Commission came out strongly in favour of increasing the amount of information to the public, and this Section reflects those wishes.

Anyone concerned with water pollution in their area should find out from their Water Authority where it keeps the register. Examination of the register will reveal five types of information;

2.22 Applications: **all applications (unless covered by an Exemption Certificate) will be found here, including those which the Authority have decided not to publicize in the local press on the grounds that the proposed discharge will have little effect. Although you have a statutory right to object only to the published Applications, it may still be worth making your views concerning other Applications known to the Water Authority.**

2.23 Consents Granted: **the list of Consents granted will give an overall picture of the discharges in your area. The register will also reveal the conditions attached to each Consent, and this should indicate whether the applicant or the Water Authority is monitoring the discharges: this last fact is most important in relation to the publicity of samples, outlined in the next paragraph. The entries will also indicate the time-table for reviewing each Consent, and this is essential information if you wish to affect an existing Consent.**

2.24 Details of Samples taken by the Water Authority: **the Water Authority is not obliged to take samples of every stretch of water in its area, but where it does, these must be published in the Register, together with information produced by analyses of the samples. But a condition attached to a Consent may provide for the Consent-holder to monitor his own discharges and pass on the results to the Authority** *(s.34(4)(e) and (f));* **this information will NOT be placed in the Register for public inspection. There is clearly a danger here that, for economic reasons, Water Authorities will be tempted to pass on the bulk of the responsibility of monitoring discharges to the dischargers themselves, and thereby cut down on information available to the public. If you** discover from examining the conditions attached to Consents that this appears to be the policy of your Water Authority, it may be worth mounting a vigorous campaign to prevent the practice spreading. Samples and analyses taken by the Authority found in the Register will provide useful information for campaigning. You may need expert help in interpreting some of the data, but, in a simple case, a discrepancy between the discharge permitted by the Consent and the discharge recorded as being made, could make embarrassing headlines for the industry concerned. Furthermore, there is nothing to prevent a private individual initiating criminal proceedings for an offence of discharging into waters without a Consent or in breach of the conditions attached to a Consent *(s.31/32)* by laying an information at the local Magistrates Court; this would be advisable only in cases where there is a clear discrepancy, and where the Water Authority is reluctant to act for some reason.

Generally, when it comes to using data obtained from the register, it must be remembered that the interpretation of pollution statistics is notoriously difficult, and it is not sensible to make play of facts discovered from the Register unless you are completely sure of your case. Be especially wary of criticizing the Water Authority on its own quality standards, unless you are confident that the discharges which they have permitted have had harmful effects.

If you have evidence of a discharge causing harm to the flora and fauna of a particular location, but discover from the Register that no samples of that stretch of water have been taken by the Authority, this could be the basis of a campaign. You should be able to pressurize the Authority into sampling, and when the results appear on the Register, this should at least provide some hard evidence about the situation.

2.25 Notices to Desist from Certain Agricultural Practices: **These Notices may be issued by the Department of the Environment to farmers requesting them to desist from activities which would be otherwise 'good agricultural practice', and a defence to proceedings under** *s.31* **(see above: 2.10). Examination of any Notices appearing in the Register may reveal the type of cases in which the Department is likely to issue such Notices, and this could be useful information for future campaigns.**

2.26 Exemption Certificates: **These Certificates, issued by the Department of the Environment, exempt the application from publicity on certain grounds (see above 2.16 & 2.27). There is little you can do to affect the granting of individual exemption certificates, since there are no publicity or consultation provisions in the procedure, and they may be issued to someone who is simply intending to make an Application some time in the future. But examination of the Certificates granted** may indicate the Department's general policy in granting certificates (though as yet it is not known just how much information will appear on the Certificates as they appear in the Register); over-indulgence by the Department in granting Exemption Certificates would be against the general spirit of the Act, and you should be prepared to campaign against this practice.

Exemption from Publicity

Section 42
Commencement Order Not Yet
(likely late 1979)
Regulations Issued Not Yet
(likely late 1979)

2.27 Under this section, Applicants may in certain situations obtain a Certificate from the Secretary of State for the Environment granting the Application exemption from the publicity provisions in the Act. A person who intends to make an Application, or who has made one, may within a period to be specified apply to the Secretary of State to grant the Certificate, and it may be granted on two grounds only:

(i) the Secretary of State is satisfied that the publicity provisions would 'prejudice to an unreasonable degree some private interest by disclosing a trade secret' *(s.42(1)(b)(i))*.

or(ii) the Secretary of State is satisfied it would be contrary to the public interest not to grant the Certificate *(s.42(1)(b)(ii))*.

Once granted, a Certificate would exempt the Application from publicity in the local press (2.15), and from being placed in the Water Register (2.15 and 2.22 above). Details of samples and analyses relating to the consented discharge would not appear on the Register, though the Exemption Certificate itself must be placed in the Register *(s.42(i)(a))*.

As explained in 2.26, you should make sure that the Department does not grant too many Exemption Certificates. It is worth noting that the disclosure of a trade secret is not in itself grounds for granting the Certificate — the disclosure must 'prejudice to an unreasonable degree some private interest'. It will be difficult to affect individual decisions, but in certain cases, you could at least request the Department to justify their action.

2.28 **Existing Consents. Under the transitional provisions relating to Consents** *(s.40),* **regulations may be made providing that consents granted under previous legislation shall continue in force as if they were Consents under this Act. This means that when the Public Register of Water Consents is first opened, you will probably find it full of consents already granted. Much of your initial work in this area is therefore likely to be trying to effect existing Consents, rather than watching for new Applications for Consents.**

2.29 The Water Authority has a duty to review all existing Consents 'from
time to time', and possesses the power to issue Notices, revoking the
Consent, or modifying or imposing new conditions. *(s.37(1))*. But each
Consent will contain a period during which no such Notice may be
served without the consent of the holder of the Consent, and this
period must be not less than **two years** *(38(1))*; similarly, following the
issue of a Notice, subsequent Notices may not be issued for another
two years at least, and so on *(38(2))*. In a few specified circumstances
the Authority may ignore this 'laying-off' period, but compensation
may be payable to the Holder if they do so.

The Secretary of State for the Environment may direct the Authority
to issue Notices of revocation or modification, and the Authority will
be legally bound by such directions. *(s.37(2))*.

**If you feel that an existing Consent should be revoked or modified,
you should first consult the Public Register since the Consent will
indicate the timing of the 'laying-off period' (see above 2.23). Where
the period has ended, press the Water Authority to review the Consent
and issue a Notice of revocation or modification; where you are
making no headway, and you feel you have a strong case, request the
Department of the Environment to exercise its powers under *s.37(2)* to
order the Authority to issue a Notice. The Authority is not legally
bound to consider the views of any objectors when they are making a
review of the Consent, nor do any publicity provisions apply to these
reviews; you will need to keep a close watch on the Register, and to
employ persuasive arguments if you are to affect these existing
Consents.**

2.30 **The 'laying-off' period must by law be a minimum of two years. It
could be longer, and a study of the Consents in the Water Register
may reveal the Water Authority's overall policy on these periods; if
you feel the average period seems excessively long, you might have the
basis of a sound campaign.**

2.31 **You may wish to affect an existing Consent within the laying-off period,
and this will probably prove quite difficult. The Authority has no legal
problems issuing a Notice within the period, provided the Consent holder
agrees; in a clear case of pollution, the holder of a Consent may be
persuaded by the thought of bad publicity to agree to tighter conditions on
the Consent.**

2.32 But there are three situations where the law allows the Water Authority to ignore this laying-off period. These are where:

(i) It is necessary to serve the Notice revoking or modifying the Consent to provide 'proper protection for persons likely to be affected' by consented discharges. *(s.37(3)(a)).* No compensation will be payable to the Consent Holder.

Even where a discharge is authorized by a Consent, riparian owners (owners of land adjoining the water) are still entitled to bring a common law action of nuisance where their waters are polluted by the discharge. This section is designed to encourage such owners to persuade the Water Authorities to revoke or modify the Consents, rather than initiate their own legal proceedings. Only where the pollution is clearly attributable to a particular source is a nuisance action likely to be successful, and in such a case, you may be able to persuade the riparian owners to make representations to the Authority to use their powers under this section. Legal advice should be sought before any legal action for nuisance is contemplated seriously.

2.33 (ii) It is appropriate to revoke or modify what is known as 'a *Section 34(3)* Consent' in consequence of objections made to the Authority. Where a discharge is made without a Consent, this would be a criminal offence (see above 2.4), but the Water Authority may, rather than initiating criminal proceedings, issue a back-dated Consent to legitimize the unauthorized discharge. This Consent, issued under *s.34(3)* may be revoked within the laying-off period, Compensation is not payble where the Notice of revocation or modification is made within 3 months of the publication of the Consent.

The Authority is probably more likely to issue these back-dated Consents than initiate criminal proceedings for unauthorized discharges. But they will be published in the local press (subject to the usual exceptions: 2.16), and it is important that you make your objections as early as possible since this will allow the Authority to revoke or modify the Consent without paying Compensation.

2.34 (iii) It appears to the Authority that pollution injurious to the flora and fauna of a stream is being caused by a consented discharge. *(s.46(1)).* If this is the case, the Authority has a duty to revoke or modify the Consent, provided this is the only solution to the problem *(s.46(2)).* Generally, compensation will not be payable, provided the Authority took the correct decision.

This is probably the most likely ground on which you will be able to affect an Existing Consent, and if you have evidence that damage to flora and fauna is being caused by a permitted discharge, campaign for

these *s.46* powers to be used. The power applies only to pollution of 'streams' (see 2.7), and will not therefore be applicable to tidal waters, underground waters and unspecified lakes or ponds which do not discharge into a stream.

GENERAL POWER TO   *Section 46*
PROTECT FLORA AND
FAUNA   Commencement Order   Not Yet
                                 (likely late 1979)
                                 Regulations Issued   Not Yet
                                 (likely late 1979)

2.35 *s.46*(1) imposes a duty on the Water Authority to 'take action' where it appears to them that pollution harmful to the flora and fauna of a stream is being caused by a permitted discharge. They must carry out work to remedy or mitigate the pollution, and, as far as practicable, restore the flora and fauna. If it is necessary to prevent further pollution, the Authority must revoke or modify the Consent, as noted above (2.34).

This section should provide useful opportunities for campaigning, although it is worth remembering that pollution that may appear to you to be harming the flora and fauna of a stream may not appear so to the Authority. But where you can present enough evidence, the Authority would have to show good reasons for taking no action at all; if they refuse to act, you can always appeal to the Secretary of State to use his powers under *s.37(2)* (see above 2.29). An Authority is unlikely to revoke or modify a Consent where it considers other remedial action (such as better filtering systems) is sufficient, especially where it is difficult to pin-point the offending discharge. Note that the Authority has a duty to restore the flora and fauna only so far as is 'practicable' a term not defined in this part of the Act; however, on an analogy with its definition in *Part IV* of the Act (Air Pollution), it includes financial as well as technical considerations, and the extent to which Authority exercises these powers will reflect policy decisions on their part.

Under *s.46(4)*, the Authority may take steps to remedy or forestall the effects of any 'poisonous, noxious or polluting matter or any solid waste' which has entered, or is likely to enter waters. This may include the removal of the waste, and, as far as practicable, the restoration of the flora and fauna. The costs of the remedial steps may be recoverable from the person responsible for the pollution.

This part of *s.46*, unlike *s.46(1)* above, is not restricted to cases where the pollution is caused by a Consented discharge. The Authority has complete discretion whether or not to act (though the Secretary of

State may order them to do so under his default powers in *section 37),* and you should note the comments about the term 'practicable' in **2.35** above. But a campaign to persuade the Authority to use its powers to improve local unsightly spots could win a great deal of local support, especially as the remedial action could include such attractions as the restocking of fish or plants.

POWER TO BAN	*Section 31(5)*
CERTAIN POLLUTING	Commencement Order Not Yet
ACTIVITIES	(likely late 1979)
	Regulations Issued Not Yet
	(likely late 1979)

2.36 The Secretary of State for the Environment has the power to ban specified activities in a particular area in order to prevent poisonous, noxious or polluting matters entering waters. *(s.31(5)* – waters are 'relevant' waters as in 2.7 above). In all cases (unless no objections were made to the proposed ban), he would first hold a local public inquiry, *(s.104(3)).*

This power is likely to be used only where all other methods of pollution control have failed. You should view it as very much a last resort when other lines of approach have not succeeded, and since it is unlikely that the Department would, for instance, shut down a local industry using these powers, the main value of a campaign under this section would lie in the publicity attached to it.

PART III: NOISE

INTRODUCTION

3.1 Until the Control of Pollution Act, most of the law on noise control was contained in the Public Health Act 1936, the Noise Abatement Act 1960 and the Public Health (Recurring Nuisances) Act 1969. These laws gave Local Authorities considerable powers to curb noises from stationary sources such as factories and houses.

Part III of the Control of Pollution Act replaces most of the existing laws, but basically re-enacts what has gone before. The Act does, however, contain one or two innovations: Local Authorities now have greater powers to prevent noise **before** it occurs; Authorities now have power to control noise from temporary construction sites; individuals, affected by noise, will now find it easier to bring proceedings in the courts; finally, Local Authorities may introduce in their area a 'Noise Abatement Zone', a new procedure, designed to hold steady and then gradually decrease existing noise levels.

The Act is mainly concerned with noise from stationary sources, and does not deal with, say, traffic or aircraft noise. TRAFFIC NOISE is controlled by regulations issued by the Department of Transport under the Road Traffic Acts 1972 and 1974[1], while AIRCRAFT NOISE is the responsibility of the Department of Trade, using its powers under the Civil Aviation Acts of 1949 and 1971.

NUISANCES   *Sections 57-9*
                       Commencement Order
                       S.I. 1975/2118
                       Regulations Issued
                       S.I. 1975/2116 (Appeals)
                       S.I. 1976/37 (Measurement)

3.2 Under *Section 57*, Local Authorities (District, or London Borough Councils) have a general duty to inspect their area from time to time to detect anything that could amount to a nuisance caused by noise.

Write to your local District or London Borough Council, asking them how they comply with their duty under *Section 57*. The reply should give some idea of their general attitude towards noise control. For instance, one local Friends of the Earth group were told by their District Council that it did not carry out special inspections, but reckoned to take notice of any nuisances they came across in the course of other duties; and they added that most nuisances caused by noise came to their notice through complaints by members of the public.

(1) Contact your local Regional Transportation Office of the Department of Transport for information (under 'Transport' in the phone book); specific complaints should be made to the police who are responsible for enforcement.

3.3 Once the Local Authority is satisfied that there is a level of noise which amounts to a nuisance, it must serve a *Notice* under *s.58* of the Act, requiring abatement of the nuisance. The type or strength of noise that amounts to a nuisance is not defined in the Act, and in the final analysis is a matter for the courts. There is a mass of court decisions concerning nuisances, and one authoritative description of a nuisance is any noise sufficient to cause 'a substantial interference with health, comfort or convenience'[1]. But the courts will take into account the locality[2], and the noise should not be merely temporary. In a recent case concerning a noisy central heating system at a block of London flats, the magistrate was reported to have said, 'I do not regard the hum as being a nuisance, but I am satisfied that the knocking or tapping sound is, especially as it clearly varies in frequency and intensity'[3].

The difficulties of defining a nuisance may explain the reluctance of many Local Authorities to issue Notices under *Section 57*. But the Secretary of State [4] has the power under the Act to issue or approve Codes of Practices on appropriate methods of noise control *(section 71)*, and it is intended to issue Codes on the best use of such troublesome devices as burglar alarms, bird scarers, and ice-cream chimes. These Codes should greatly help Local Authorities in assessing whether or not a particular noise amounts to a nuisance.

A Local Authority may also issue a Notice under *section 58* where, though there is no nuisance at present, they are satisfied that a nuisance is 'likely to occur or reoccur'. The words 'to occur' did not appear in previous legislation on noise control, and their presence represents an important extension of the powers of Local Authorities in that they can now prevent a nuisance before it takes place.

The Notice is served on the person responsible for the noise, or, if he or she cannot be found, on the owner or occupier of the premise from which the noise is emitted. Failure to comply with the Notice is a criminal offence, but where the noise occurred in the course of a trade of business, it will be a valid defence in court proceedings to show that the 'best practicable means had been used to comply with the notice.' This phrase is given a broad definition in *s.72* of the Act[5], but it will be up to the courts to interpret the phrase precisely.

---

(1) Vanderpant v Mayfair Hotel Co. Ltd (1930) 1 Ch. 138.
(2) 'What would be a nuisance in Belgrave Square would not necessarily be so in Bermondsey' – Sturges v Bridgman (1879) 2 Ch. D 852,865 per Thesiger J.
(3) Reported in the Kensington Post, 1.4.77.
(4) The Secretary of State for the Environment, in practice.
(5) 'practicable' is defined as 'reasonably practicable having regard among other things to local conditions and circumstances, to the current state of technical knowledge and to the financial implications' (*s.72(2)*).

A person served with a Notice may within 21 days appeal to the Magistrates Court, but where a person fails to abate the noise (because he is making an appeal or simply waiting for the Local Authority to initiate court proceedings), the Local Authority may apply to the High Court for an injunction to stop the noise in the meantime *(s.58(8))*[1]. An application for an injunction is likely to be made only in extreme cases: before the Court will grant such an injunction, the Authority must give an undertaking in damages, and if it is later shown that they acted prematurely or unnecessarily, the damages will be payable as compensation.

If you feel that the noise from premises in your area is excessive, ask the Environmental Health Department of your District Council to issue a Notice under *Section 58*. **Find out from the District Council whether an Environmental Health Officer will be available after office hours to deal with such problems as late night parties, night-time industry or ringing burglar-alarms. Remember that the Council may take action before the nuisance occurs, so if you know of plans for the expansion of a noisy activity, you could ask the Council to issue a Notice requiring the noise to be kept within a certain limit.**

3.4 An occupier of premises may himself initiate court proceedings if he is 'aggrieved by noise amounting to a nuisance' *(s.59)*. The individual must apply to the local Magistrates Court, who, after considering the case, may then issue an Order. This has a similar effect to the Section 58 Notice issued by the Local Authority, and failure to comply with the Court Order is a criminal offence.[2] Under previous legislation, three persons had to apply the Court, so individuals will now find it easier to start court action.

But unlike the Local Authority's powers under *s.58,* this section applies only to *existing* noises, though the Court has the power to issue an Order where it is satisfied that the nuisance, though abated at the time of the court proceedings, is likely to recur on the same premises.

If your District Council is unwilling to take action under *s.58,* **you can apply yourself to the Magistrates Court under** *s.59,* **provided you are an occupier of premises[3], which is adversely affected by the noise. Contact the Clerk of your local Magistrates Court (under 'Courts' in**

---

(1) The Appeal Court recently confirmed that an injunction could be granted in the High Court, despite concurrent appeal proceedings in the Magistrates Court: Hammersmith London Borough Council v Magnum Automated Forecourts Ltd (1978) 1 AER 401.
(2) though, as under s.58, if the noise occurred in the course of trade or business, it will be a good defence to show that the 'best practicable means' had been used to prevent, or counteract the effect of the noise *(s.59(5))*.
(3) an 'occupier' includes both the owner, and a tenant, and, possibly, a squatter.

the 'phone book) for details of the procedure. There is no charge for the application to the Court, though if you lost the case, the Court might decide that you should pay the defendant's costs. This is up to the discretion of Court, and if you convinced them of the reasonableness of your action,[1] they would probably not make an award against you. The Action under *s.59* is likely to be especially appropriate where the offender is the Council itself, since an Environmental Health Department will probably be unwilling to initiate against another Department of the Council. The first action under *s.59* was taken by a council tenant against Hackney Council, and concerned a noisy boiler in his block of flats, and in April 1977 a 77 year old pensioner was successful in an action against the G.L.C. over a noisy central heating system in his council flat.

3.5 **Government Buildings etc:** *Part III* of the Act does not apply to Crown Premises (which include all Government Buildings), but it does cover premises belonging to public corporations, such as the National Coal Board or British Rail, other than those belong to one of the national health corporations.[2] Local Authorities do have to comply with the Act.

CONSTRUCTION SITES   *Sections 60–61*

Commencement Order S.I. 1975/2118
Regulations Issued S.I. 1975/2115

3.6 Under previous law, local authorities could not control the noise coming from temporary construction sites, or where the work was being carried out with reasonable care to prevent unnecessary annoyance. The new provisions in the Control of Pollution Act give local authorities greater powers to regulate this source of noise.

Under *section 60,* a local authority may serve a notice requiring noise on a particular construction site to be kept within a certain limit or work to be carried out at specified hours, but a person about to carry out construction work may protect himself by applying beforehand for a consent to make a specified level of noise. In considering whether or not to issue a notice, or the granting of a consent, the local authority is obliged to have regard to the approved code of practice[3] (*section 60(4) and 61(5)*). Finally, the Secretary of State has the power to make regulations limiting the noise levels that are emitted from plant and machinery used on construction sites, but he must ensure that such

(1) your 'reasonableness' should include attempts to persuade those causing the noise to take the necessary action to stop the noise before you launch in with court proceedings. You should be able to produce copies of letters you wrote to those responsible.

(2) Garner, Control of Pollution Encyclopaedia, 1.53.

(3) Control of noise (Code of practice for Construction Sites) order 1975, S.I. 1975/2115.

NUISANCE PROCEDURE

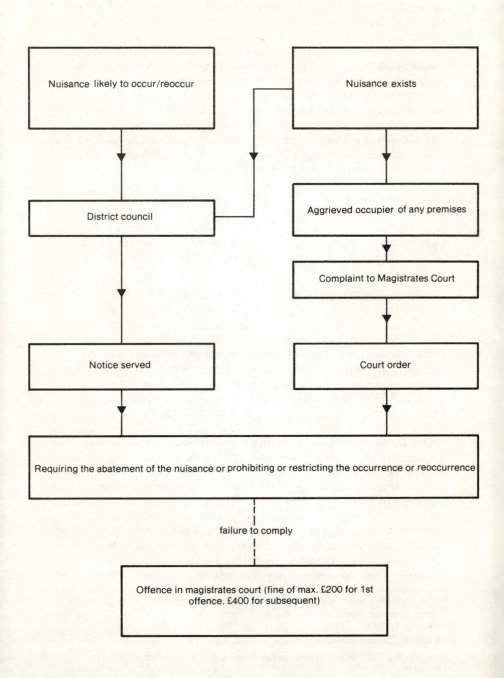

Nuisance likely to occur/reoccur

Nuisance exists

District council

Aggrieved occupier of any premises

Complaint to Magistrates Court

Notice served

Court order

Requiring the abatement of the nuisance or prohibiting or restricting the occurrence or reoccurrence

failure to comply

Offence in magistrates court (fine of max. £200 for 1st offence, £400 for subsequent)

regulations would not be impracticable or involve unreasonable expense *(section 68(1)(b) and (2))*.

Where you are troubled by a noise construction site, or hear of a planned construction works, ask your District Council whether or not they intend to serve a notice under section 60, or grant a consent if they receive an application from the operator. If a consent has already been granted, what noise levels are specified? Does the consent specify hours of working? But remember that the council is not obliged to use its powers under these sections, nor are they under any legal duty to make public the details of specific consents or notices.

NOISE ABATEMENT ZONES *Sections 63–67*

Commencement Order S.1. 1975/2118
Regulations Issued S.1. 1976/37

3.7 Under the Act, local authorities (District/London Borough Councils) now have the discretionary power to designate any area a 'Noise Abatement Zone', a concept totally new in noise legislation. The object of a Noise Abatement Zone is to hold steady, and then gradually reduce the noise levels in a particular area, and this area may cover the size of a single factory site right up to the whole of the local authority's area.

While the power to designate zones is discretionary, the Local Authority has a legal duty under *s.57* to carry out inspections from time to time into the possibility of establishing zones.

Before a zone is designated, the necessary Order – a Noise Abatement Order – has to go to the Secretary of State for the Environment for confirmation, and he may, if he feels a need, call a local inquiry at which objections and representations may be made.[1] The Noise Abatement Order will specify certain classes of premises within the area chosen, and it is the noise from these premises which will be controlled and eventually reduced by the procedure. The Department of the Environment have suggested to Local Authorities six classes of premises[2] as suitable for specification, and these include industrial premises, commercial premises, entertainment establishments, agricultural premises, transport installations, and public utility installations; domestic premises have been excluded from the suggested list, and the D.O.E. advise that the control of noise from dwellings is best achieved by the use of the nuisance powers under *s.58/59*.

(1) The D.O.E. have produced a booklet 'Noise Abatement Zone Inquiries – What you need to know' – free of charge from D.O.E., Room 481, Queen Annes Chambers, 28 Broadway, London SW1.

(2) D.O.E. Circular 2/76, Implementation of Part III Control of Pollution Act, No. 1.

Establishing a Noise Abatement Zone is both a novel and expensive procedure for Local Authorities, and at the time of writing only ten Orders had been confirmed by the Secretary of State. As yet, it is impossible to say in what cases a Zone will be most effective and appropriate, though the D.O.E. have advised it may be particularly suitable for large-scale plans for mixed residential and industrial development. They have also suggested that Local Authorities should consider establishing small-scale experimental Zones in order to give them experience in the new procedures.

It is worth finding out if your District Council has developed a policy on Noise Abatement Zones. You might first write to the Council's Environmental Health Department, asking them in what way they are carrying out their duties of inspections under *s.57* into the possibility of establishing zones, and whether they have any firm plans or policies yet.

One local Friends of the Earth Group received a long reply from the City Health Officer, explaining in detail why the Authority felt the use of Noise Abatement Zones was a waste of time and money. Where a Local Authority pleads lack of financial resources, suggest they designate a small pilot zone, as recommended by the Department of the Environment. There are no public consultation procedures written into the Noise Abatement Zone provisions, and if you want to play a part in the designation of a Zone (you may, for example, want a particular type of premises classified), you will have to establish good relations with the Environmental Health Officers of your local Council to make sure you keep in touch with developments. A campaign for the establishment of a Noise Abatement Zone will be particularly appropriate where you discover that planning permission for large-scale industrial development is being sought, especially when residential areas are likely to be affected. Before confirming a Noise Abatement Order, the Secretary of State may hold a public local inquiry, where you would be able to make formal representations. If you feel anxious about some part of the proposed Order, campaign for the Secretary of State to hold an inquiry before confirmation.[1]

3.8   Once the Noise Abatement Zone has been established, the local authority must measure the existing noise levels in the area, in accordance with detailed regulations issued by the Secretary of State.[2]

---

(1) In January 1978, the Department of the Environment approved a Noise Abatement Order in Hammersmith despite the recommendation against it by the Inspector at the Inquiry. According to a D.O.E. spokesman, 'Confirmation of the Order means that the Government wants to push for establishment of noise abatement zones even though the law is discretionary'.

(2) Control of Noise (Measurements and Registers) Regulations 1976 (1976/37).

Noise Abatement Order

THE *

(hereinafter called " the Council ") in exercise of the powers conferred upon them by section 63 of the Control of Pollution Act 1974 HEREBY make the following order:

1. This Order shall be cited as the

.   Noise Abatement Order 19

2. The area which is coloured   on the map prepared in duplicate, sealed with the Common Seal of the Council and marked " Map referred to in the

.   Noise Abatement Order, 19   "

is hereby declared to be a Noise Abatement Zone. One duplicate of the map is deposited in the offices of the Council at

and the other is deposited in the offices of the Secretary of State for the Environment.

3. This Order relates to premises of the classes described in the Schedule hereto.

4. Within the area coloured   on the map, the premises coloured

.   are the premises identified by the Council as being premises to which this Order will relate when brought into operation.

5. This Order shall come into operation   months from the date of confirmation by the Secretary of State.

SCHEDULE

Classes of Premises

Given under the Seal of the Council this   day of   19

(L.S.)

---

* Insert name of local authority.

These regulations specify the precise methods and units of measurements to be used (the basic measurement is the equivalent continuous noise level (Leq) measured in dB(A), and a local authority that wishes to use other methods must secure the permission of the Secretary of State.[1]

3.9 The measurements that are made must then be entered on a Public Register (the 'Noise Level Register'), which must specify the date and time of the measurements, the location and height of the points at which they were made, details of equipment used, and the weather conditions. Once the noise measurements have been entered on the Register, it becomes an offence to exceed those levels, without prior consent of the local authority (*s.65(1) and (5)*). In granting a consent to exceed the level, the authority may attach conditions as to when and by how much the level of noise may be increased, and the details of any consent must be entered on the Noise Level Register.

Find out from your local authority where the Noise Level Register is kept. It must be open to the public at reasonable hours, and members of the public must be able to obtain copies of entries at reasonable charges.[2] Where an occupier appears to be exceeding the registered noise levels, or overlooking the conditions attached to a Consent, report the matter to the Environmental Health Officer. The Authority is under no legal obligation to investigate a complaint made in this way, but the DOE had advised that 'local authorities will obviously wish to monitor noise levels when complaints about noise from classified premises are received.'[3] Measurements that you make yourself (with, say, the help of a local polytechnic or technical college) will clearly add weight to a case, but, unless the detailed procedure outlined in the regulations has been carefully followed (see above 3.8), they are unlikely to be conclusive, and in most situations it will be better to persuade the local authority to perform the measurements itself, and prove the case for you. Where a local authority fails to respond to your complaints, you may still initiate a nuisance action in the local Magistrates Court under *s.59* (see above 3.4), provided you are an occupier of premises affected by the noise. The fact that the level of noise is in accordance with a Consent issued by the Local Authority is of itself no defence to a nuisance action (*s.65(8)*), though it may well bear some weight with the court.

3.10 The procedure described above allows a local authority to hold steady the existing noise levels in the Noise Abatement Zone, but the real

---

(1) ibid, *s.4(2)*.

(2) *s.64(7)*.

(3) *D.O.E. Circular 2/76 'Implementation of Part III Control of Pollution Act'.*

point of the whole procedure is to reduce gradually the noise levels in the area. Where a local authority feels that the existing noise levels are not acceptable, and that a reduction is practicable at reasonable cost, and 'would afford a public benefit', it may issue a Notice requiring the occupier of the premises to reduce the levels of noise to a new level specified in the Notice *(s.66)*. This is an important power, new to local authorities, and allows them great flexibility in slowly reducing noise levels in a Noise Abatement Zone. The Noise Reduction Notice does not necessarily have to require a blanket reduction of the noise level, but may specify a reduction at certain times (nights or weekends, for example), or even the noise coming from a particular part of the premises. Details of any Noise Reduction Notice must be entered on the Noise Level Register (see above 3.9). An occupier, served with a Noise Reduction Notice, may appeal within 3 months to the local Magistrates Court on certain grounds specified in regulations issued by the Secretary of State.[1] Failure to comply with a Notice is an offence, though it will be good defence in any proceedings to prove that the 'best practicable means' had been used to prevent, or counteract the effect of the noise.

Where you feel that, within a Noise Abatement Zone, the noise levels on the Public Register are higher than they should be for certain premises, campaign for the local authority to issue a Noise Reduction Notice. In many cases, this may be simpler and quicker than attempting to start nuisance proceedings in the courts, though it should always be remembered that a local authority has no legal obligation to take into consideration any representations from the public on these matters, and its powers under section 66 are entirely discretionary.

NOISE IN STREETS

Section 62
COMMENCEMENT ORDER 1975
S.I. 1975/2118
NO REGULATIONS REQUIRED

3.11 The Control of Pollution Act is concerned mainly with noise from stationary sources such as factories or dwellings. Noise in streets is generally controlled by local by-laws, but *s.62* provides special controls over the use of loudspeakers in the streets. Generally, loudspeakers cannot be operated in a street between 9 p.m. and 8 a.m. (with exceptions for the use of loudspeakers by the police, firebrigade and other services), and, in addition, loudspeakers may not be used at any time in streets for the purpose of advertising an entertainment, trade

---

(1) Control of Noise (Appeals) Regulations 1975 (1975 S.I. 2216), s.7.

or business. The only exception in the latter case is for loudspeakers attached to ice-cream vans (or other vans carrying 'a perishable commodity for human consumption'), which may be operated between noon and 7 p.m., provided they do not cause an annoyance to people in the vicinity. These controls are a re-enactment of those contained in previous legislation, though the penalties have been much increased.

Where the use of loudspeakers in the streets is causing a disturbance, complaints should be made to the Environmental Health Officer of your District or London Borough Council. Check with the Officer whether there are any extra by-laws in force, controlling the use of loudspeakers.

PART IV: AIR

INTRODUCTION

4.1 This part of the Act is not nearly as comprehensive as the sections on land, water and noise, as the major sources of air pollution are covered by existing legislation.[1]

4.2 SMOKE, from both domestic and industrial sources, is controlled by the Environmental Health Departments of District and London Borough Councils, using their powers under the Clean Air Acts of 1956 and 1968. These acts forbid the emission of what is known as 'dark smoke'[2], and, in addition, the local authorities may create Smoke Control Areas (popularly known as 'smokeless zones'), after which the use of certain types of fuel in that area becomes an offence. It was the use of this legislation which was so successful in ridding London of its smog problem of the 1950's.

4.3 NOXIOUS OR OFFENSIVE GASES, including smoke, grit and dust from certain specified industrial processes, are controlled by the Alkali Inspectorate, a government body. Once the process becomes specified — and the list now includes much of the chemical, refining, electricity and metal manufacturing industries — the local authority loses all jurisdiction, even in smokeless zones. The Alkali Inspectorate act under the Alkali, etc. Works Regulation Act 1906 and subsequent legislation, and are now part of the Health and Safety Executive (Baynards House, 1–13 Chepstow Place, Westbourne Grove, London W1). In the past, the Inspectorate has been heavily criticized for being secretive, uncooperative with local authorities, and too lenient towards factory polluters.[3] The First Report of the Royal Commission on Environmental Pollution (HMSO Cmnd 4585, 1971) recommended a vigorous application of the Alkali Act, and the Government responded by substantially increasing the number of inspectors.[4] The Control of Pollution Act makes no changes to the present arrangements in this area.

---

(1) see, for instance, 'Clean Air — Law and Practice' by Garner and Crow (Shaw & Sons Ltd. 1976).

(2) defined as smoke 'dark as, or darker than' Shade 2 on the Ringelmann Chart.

(3) for the definitive critical work, see 'The Alkali Inspectorate', Social Audit Special Report 1974 (Social Audit, 9 Poland St, London W1).

(4) p. 15, 'Controlling Pollution', Pollution Paper No. 4 (HMSO 1975).

4.4   EXHAUST FUMES from motor vehicles are controlled by regulations
made by the Department of Transport under the Road Traffic Act
1972. The controls are enforced by the police.[1]

4.5   *Part IV* of the Control of Pollution Act gives the Government power
to regulate the composition of certain fuels; creates a new offence of
'cable-burning'; and gives local authorities new powers of collecting
information on problems of air pollution.

PREVENTION OF POLLUTION *Sections 75–77*

Commencement Order 1975/2118
Regulations Issued 1976/1866
1976/1988
1976/1989

4.6   *s.75* allows the Secretary of State for Transport to regulate the
composition of fuel used in motor vehicles. Before making any
regulations, the Secretary of State is obliged to consult representatives
of vehicle manufacturers, vehicle users, motor fuel manufacturers, and
persons 'conversant with problems of air pollution', as he considers
appropriate *(s.75(2))*. Two sets of regulations have already been made,
prescribing maximum levels for the lead content in petrol, and for the
sulphur content of diesel fuel.[2] The Secretary of State for the
Environment has similar powers under *s.76* to regulate the sulphur
content of oil fuels used in furnaces or engines, and a set of
regulations was made in 1976.[3] Sulphur dioxide, the product of
combustion of sulphur in sulphur-rich fuels, can be a local hazard, and
emissions from power stations, using low-grade fuels, can be especially
high.

CABLE-BURNING   *Section 78*

Commencement Order 1975/2118
Regulations — None Required

4.7   *Section 78* makes the process of cable-burning an offence, unless
carried out on premises registered under the Alkali Acts, and thereby
under the supervision of the Alkali Inspectorate. Cable-burning is an
industry performed often on a small-scale by entrepreneurs who burn
off insulation from cable to recover the metal. It can cause smoke and

---

(1) Requests for information can be made to the Vehicle Standards and Engineering
Division, Department of Transport, 2 Marsham St., London SW1; complaints concerning
individual vehicles should be made to the local police.

(2) Motor Fuel (Lead Content of Petrol) Regulations 1976 (1976 S.1. 1866).
Motor Fuel (Sulphur Content of Gas Oil) Regulations 1976 (1976 S.1. 1989).

(3) Oil Fuel (Sulphur Content of Gas Oil) Regulations 1976 (1976 S.1. 1988).

noxious fumes, and there had been legal doubts about the effectiveness of either the Alkali Acts or the Clean Air Acts in controlling the problem. *Section 78* removes the doubts. Proceedings for an offence under this section may be instituted only by an Inspector appointed under the Health & Safety at Work etc. Act 1974, or by or with the consent of the Director of Public Prosecutions.[1]

INFORMATION AND RESEARCH	*Sections 79–83* Commencement Order 1975/2118 Regulations Issued 1977/17 (Appeals) 1977/18 (Exempted premises) 1977/19 (Research & Publicity)

4.8 These sections authorize District or London Borough Councils to undertake research into air pollution problems, and will be the sections affording most opportunity to groups campaigning in this area. But the powers of the local authorities are entirely discretionary, and 'in the light of the continuing restraints on local authority expenditure it will be difficult for authorities who wish to make use of the powers to find the necessary resources from within their existing budget.' (DOE Circular 2/77, para. 2).

Anyone campaigning in this area should remember that the local authorities have no legal duty to undertake research under these sections. Arguments about the need for such research will have to be especially persuasive, since an authority would have to cut down resources in other areas of its expenditure if it is to use these powers.

4.9 Under *section 79,* the local authority has general powers to undertake or fund research into problems of air pollution, and to arrange for the publication of information on the subject, provided no trade secrets are breached (*s.79(5)*). In particular they may enter into arrangements with the occupiers of premises (other than private dwellings) for the measuring and recording of emissions into the air. They may not make such arrangements with occupiers of premises already supervised by the Alkali Inspectorate (see above 4.3). Where they require information about such premises, or where an occupier of other premises is unwilling to supply information, the authority must issue a formal Notice under the following section.

4.10 Under *section 80,* the local authority possess a new power to issue Notices requiring the occupiers of premises (other than private dwellings) to supply information on emissions into the air. This is subject to the proviso that where the premises are already under the

---

(1) *s. 78* as amended by Clean Air Enactments (Repeals and Modifications) Regulations 1974 (SI 1974/2170).

supervision of the Alkali Inspectorate, the local authority may obtain only the same information being supplied to the Inspectorate. But in such a case, the local authority, unlike the Inspectorate, will be bound to publish the information obtained in the Public Register (see below 4.12).

Regulations have now been issued prescribing the manner in which local authorities are to exercise this power.[1] The Notice may require the following types of information:

(1) The total amount of sulphur dioxide discharged over a specified period, and the time for which discharges of sulphur dioxide were made within that period, together with certain technical details of the emission (temperature, flow rate, height of chimney etc.).

(2) The total amount of particulate matter emitted within a specified period, the time for which such discharges were made and the concentration of particulate matter in released gases, together with the technical details as in (1).

(3) For any other specified gas, or specified particulate matter information as in (2).

The information required must relate to emissions from 'any chimney flue or other outlet' (*s.3* of the 1977 regulations) and a Notice may not relate to a period of more than 12 months. If the Authority is seeking information relating to *past* emissions, it may require only information which the occupier has at hand already (*s. 4(2)* of the regulations). It is therefore probable that most Notices will require information relating to emissions that will take place over the next twelve months (or a shorter period) since this will give the occupier time to instal suitable monitoring equipment.

Many local authorities will already be obtaining data on industrial emissions, but these new formal powers of issuing Notices will be especially useful where an industry has been unwilling or recalcitrant in supplying information in the past. Failure to comply with the requirements in a Notice is a summary offence, with a maximum fine of £400 (*s. 80(7)(a)*).

A group intending to campaign in this area should first write to the Environmental Health Officer of their District or London Borough Council, to find out what action his department is at present taking to obtain information on problems of air pollution in the area. Will the Authority be using its new powers under the Control of Pollution Act, and does it intend to issue Notices under *section 80?* Suitable premises on which Notices should be served could be suggested.

(1) Control of Atmosphere Pollution (Research and Publicity) Regulations 1977 (SI 1977/19) and DOE Circular 2/77.

4.11 **Appeals against Notices:** Within 6 weeks of receiving a *section 80* Notice[1] the occupier of the premises must furnish the information. Alternatively, he may appeal to the Secretary of State for the Environment that he should not be obliged to furnish the information on any of the following,grounds:

(a) he would be prejudiced to an unreasonable degree because the information would disclose a trade secret.

(b) disclosure to the public would be contrary to the public interest.

(c) he would incur undue expenditure in supplying the information required.

Details of the appeal procedure are now laid down in regulations[2], and the Secretary of State could hold a local inquiry into the matter before deciding the appeal.[3]

The local authority are not obliged to publicize details of Notices issued, or appeals lodged. The information might be obtained from a friendly councillor or officer, and, where a group has discovered that an appeal has been made against the Notice, they should write to the Department of the Environment, explaining why the appeal should be dismissed. Where the issue is of sufficient local importance, a campaign for a local inquiry could be mounted.

4.12 **Public Registers:** Once a local authority decides to exercise its powers under this part of the Act, it must set up a Public Register, containing the information obtained from *section 80* Notices, or from the use of the Authority's general powers under *section 79* .[4] The regulations covering the setting up of these Public Registers do not specify in detail the form of the register, but the register must be adequately indexed to allow the information relating to particular premises to be found easily.[5] Details of appeals against *section 80* Notices which have been allowed by the Secretary of State must also be entered on the register. The Local Authority must allow the public to obtain copies of entries, on payment of reasonable charges. (*s. 82(5)*).

---

(1) or longer if the local authority specifies.

(2) Control of Atmosphere Pollution (Appeals Regulations 1977 (SI 1977/17)).

(3) using his general power to hold local inquiries under s. 96 (cf below 5.1).

(4) s. 82 (5) and Control of Atmospheric Pollution (Research and Publicity) Regulations 1977 (SI 1977/19), *s.6.*

(5) ibid.

Where a local authority has decided to exercise its powers under this part of the Act, a group should find out where and when the public register will be available for inspection.

A study of the Register should provide useful raw data on the substances being emitted in your area. But, unless you have access to someone with the expertise to interpret this information, you will not learn from the register what impact the emissions are having at ground level: this will greatly depend on the nature of the particular pollutants and local meteorological conditions.

But the Register should clearly reveal areas lacking in information, and where there are no entries for particularly troublesome premises, a group should persuade the local authority to seek the information, and, if necessary, issue a section 80 Notice.

4.13 **Consultative Committees:** Where a local authority plans to exercise any of the powers under this part of the Act, it must from 'time to time' consult local representatives of industry, together with persons appearing to the authority to be 'conversant with problems of air pollution' and with persons appearing to have an 'interest in the amenity' (*s. 79(8)*). The Department of the Environment in Circular 2/77 has advised local authorities that these consultations can be best conducted through the establishment of local committees, and that these committees should be set up before the authority embarks on any programme of research in order to achieve cooperation from local industry and to assess the strength of local opinion on the issues.

A local group, with a good track record, should at an early stage find out whether their local authority intends to follow the Department's advice to set up such a committee. The group should request to be included, even when it knows that the local authority does not yet intend to use its powers under the Act. One local Friends of the Earth Group made such a request, and were informed by the Environmental Health Officer that, if at some time in the future the authority did exercise its powers under the Act, and set up a consultative committee, 'I can assure you that your Group will be contacted and asked to nominate a member to sit on such a Committee.'

Another local group discovered that their local authority felt there was no need for a consultative committee under *s. 79* since they had already established a liaison committee with the major industry in the area, an aluminium smelters. Such liaison committees are fairly common, and while they may be a convenient arrangement for the authority to gain access to details of emissions, they should not be thought of as a substitute for *s. 79* committees. Members of liaison committees are often sworn to secrecy by the industry, and representatives of outside bodies are unlikely to be invited to join. If your Council is quite satisfied with the arrangements of a local liaison committee, it may be worth working through the opposition party on the Council on the lines that the party in power has created a system that suppresses important information from public scrutiny.

4.14 **Reserve powers of Government:** Finally, under section 83 of the Act, the Secretary of State has the power to direct a local authority to install and operate equipment for measuring air pollution, and to send the information so obtained to him. The Secretary of State must defray the capital cost of equipment required under his direction. (*s. 83(2)*).

A local authority may be unwilling to investigate particular air pollution problems, especially if a high capital expenditure will be required. Where the problem is of more than local significance — for instance, the lead emissions at a large motorway interchange — a group could campaign for the Department of the Environment to issue a direction under *s.83,* **and thereby defray the capital costs of the research.**

PART V: GENERAL POWERS

5.1   LOCAL INQUIRIES

5.2   DEFAULT POWERS OF GOVERNMENT

5.3   POWER TO BAN USE OF POLLUTING
                SUBSTANCES

5.1　**LOCAL INQUIRIES**　　*Section 96*
Commencement Order S.1. 1975/2118
No regulations required

The Secretary of State has power under *section 96* to hold an inquiry in any case which he considers appropriate in connection with a provision in the Control of Pollution Act, or with a view to preventing or dealing with pollution or noise generally.

This is a wide, discretionary power to hold an inquiry into virtually any case concerning pollution. It should provide a useful basis for a campaign, and will be appropriate where the existing provisions in the legislation have clearly failed to provide proper controls, or to allow a full examination of the issues and facts surrounding the case.

5.2　**DEFAULT POWERS OF**　　*Secretary 97*
　　　SECRETARY OF STATE　Commencement Order S.1. 1975/2118
No regulations required

Under this Section, the Secretary of State has power to make an Order declaring an Authority to be in default of its duties under any provision of the Control of Pollution Act. The Order may direct the Authority to carry out the duty, and if it fails to comply with the direction, The Secretary of State may carry out the particular functions and charge the cost to the Authority.

A large number of the Sections in the Act impose legal duties on the Authorities concerned, and where you feel an Authority is not fulfilling its duties properly, you should request the Department of the Environment to issue (or threaten to) an Order under *section 97*. But remember that there is a clear distinction between an Authority's legal duties and its discretionary powers.

5.3　**POWER TO PREVENT THE**　*Section 100*
　　　USE OR IMPORTATION OF　Commencement Order S.1. 1975/2119
　　　POLLUTING SUBSTANCES　Regulations not required

Section 100 gives the Secretary of State the power to issue regulations that restrict or prohibit
(a) the importation of any substance
or (b) the use of any substance in connection with any trade or business
or (c) the supply of any substance for any purpose.

But he must be satisfied that it is appropriate to issue such regulations to prevent the substance causing damage to persons, animal or plant life, or pollution of air, water or land. Before making such regulations, he must give notice of their intended effect and consider any representations made to him.

Again, *Section 100* **gives the Department of the Environment a very wide discretion to take action to prevent pollution, and it is one that is likely to be used sparingly. Where existing controls are proving ineffective, this section could provide the basis of a good campaign — if your case is strong, the fact that the Department has these powers means they would have to justify publicly their reasons for not exercising them.**

APPENDIX I

BIBLIOGRAPHY

The literature on the various aspects of pollution and its control is scattered and diffuse. It ranges from more or less specialised books and reports discussing the extent and effect of pollution to those dealing with economic, social and political aspects of pollution, to books purely on pollution control technology.

A good deal of information is published in reports of government departments and committees and in the specialised scientific press. HMSO supply most of the government publications and the scientific journals may be consulted in university and college libraries. Library classification systems tend not to include a 'pollution' classmark. Be prepared to look under 'ecology', 'public health', 'engineering & technology', 'law and 'economics' classmarks.

The bibliography below is far from comprehensive, but should provide the reader with a start in the search for further information. It is divided into "technical" and "legal" sections, although there are inevitably items which are not susceptible to this categorisation.

A. TECHNICAL BIBLIOGRAPHY

Industrial Pollution (N. I. Sax, editor, Van Nostrand Reinhold, New York, 1974), is a mine of information on all types of pollution. At £22.75 (1976 prices) it is to be consulted in public libraries rather than purchased, but its 677 pages and 100 page appendix on pollutants and their properties are extremely useful to anybody trying to find out about any particular hazard and the ability of the environment to tolerate, degrade and disperse it. *Social Audit's Pollution Handbook* (M Frankel, Macmillan published September, 1978) provides an invaluable lay person's guide to toxic hazards occurring in and around the workplace. A readily purchasable and digestible introduction to the effects of various pollutants is provided by *The Biology of Pollution* (K. Mellanby, Edward Arnold for the Institute of Biology). A book dealing more specifically with the control of pollution — covering legal, technical and economic aspects is *Industrial Pollution Control* (K. A. Tearle, Business Books Ltd 1973).

A number of publications are available which deal in detail with air, water and noise pollution. Pollution in the Air (R. S. Scorer, Routledge 1973) covers issues of atmospheric pollution. Always of interest are the annual Reports of the *Alkali etc Works Inspectorate* (HMSO for the Health & Safety Exec), which should be read in conjunction with Social Audit's report *The Alkali Inspectorate — The Control of Industrial Air Pollution* (Social Audit Special Report, 1974).

Two government publications describe the current state of water pollution and the research effort going into controlling and understanding it. These are: *The River Pollution Survey of England & Wales* (HMSO 1975) and *Water Pollution Research 1973* (HMSO 1976). Also worth consulting are the Annual Reports of the local Regional Water Authority which should be available in public libraries within the relevant region. The Water Research Centre (Stevenage, Herts) has most comprehensive library and bibliographic services covering water resources management, including pollution and its control.

A useful book for those dealing with a noise problem is *Noise* (R. Taylor, Penguin Books 2nd edition 1975).

Two series of government reports supply information on general aspects of pollution. Firstly the Royal Commission on Environmental Pollution has published six reports:
First Report (Cmmd 4585 1971)
2nd, *Three Issues in Pollution Control* (Cmmd 4894, 1972)
3rd, *Pollution of Esturies and Coastal Waters* (Cmmd 5054, 1972)
4th, *Pollution Control, Progress and Problems* (Cmmd 5780 1974)
5th, *Air Pollution Control — an integrated Approach* (Cmmd 6371 1976)
6th, *Nuclear Power and the Environment* (Cmmd 6618 1976)
The commission is presently studying agriculture and pollution and is expected to report on this topic soon.

The second series of reports are those of the DoE's Central Unit on Environmental Pollution, among the more interesting are:-

No. 1 Monitoring of the Environment in the UK.
No. 2 Lead in the environment and its significance to man.
No. 3 Non-agricultural uses of pesticides in Great Britain.
No. 9 Pollution Control in Great Britain: How it works.
This last report is a DoE reply to the reports (above) of the Royal Commission, and contains a useful summary of the various administrative and legal arrangements for dealing with pollution, both within and outside of the framework of the Control of Pollution Act.
New Scientist, Nature and *Science* often carry articles on pollution, its effects and monitoring programmes. A number of journals deal with pollution specifically. *Environmental Pollution* (Applied Sciences Publishers, London) carries many articles on the biological effects of pollution, *Pollution Abstracts* (Date Courier Inc, Louisville, Kentucky) lists articles, with short abstracts from 2,500 sources under air, water, noise etc sections. More specialist are *Marine Pollution Bulletin* (Pergamon Press) and *Clean Air* (Journal of the National Society for Clean Air).

B. LEGAL BIBLIOGRAPHY

A readable guidebook to the law and environmental policy is *Law and Administration relating to the Protection of the Environment* (D. A. Bingham Oyez 1973, plus supplement updating to 1.12.74).

The most comprehensive legal text on pollution is the *Control of Pollution Encyclopaedia* (J. F. Garner 1977 (£33!)), loose-leaf format practitioners work, containing all relevant statutes and regulations. The same author has three other useful works, An annotated version of the *Control of Pollution Act* (Butterworths annotated legal documents 1975) *Clean Air — Law & Practice* (Shaw, 4th edition 1976) and Law on Sewers and Drains (Shaw 1975).

The legal handbook on noise pollution is *The Law relating to Noise* (C. S. Kerse, Oyez 1975).

APPENDIX II

MAKING REPRESENTATIONS

Throughout the Control of Pollution Act. there are opportunities for individuals and groups to make representations to the appropriate authorities be it the local District Council or the Secretary of State for the Environment. These representations can have a key effect on the decision-making process, and while the content of an objection is, of course, a matter for the individual concerned, its layout and style can greatly increase its effectiveness. Many amenity groups and individuals now have considerable experience in the art of making such representations, and these notes are meant to guide someone who has become involved in these issues for the first time.

i. Make sure you address the objection to the correct Department, and notice of applications etc. will often quote the name of an individual officer to whom objections should be made. If necessary ring up the Authority to check details.

ii. Always quote the reference number of an Application, if it is given.

iii. Objections should be typed and double-spaced, with a summary of the points to be made.

iv. Give details of your interest in the application; e.g. that you are a resident in property neighbouring to the site in question. Where a group makes an objection, it should describe its general aims and membership size (though membership size is far less important than the quality of the objection).

v. Give as much factual support (including references to documents, where appropriate) to your arguments as possible.

iv. Where you have to make objections within a statutory period, and you are hard pressed for time, it is often sufficient to send a summary of your objections within the period; this can be followed later by the detailed supporting arguments. But always ring up the appropriate Authority first, if you think this will be necessary.

vii. Keep copies of all your correspondence.

To give an idea of the nature of objections, we have included (opposite) what might be a typical objection to the granting of a Waste Disposal Site:

Talboth Friends of Wessex

J Fawley Esq
Dept A/106
Wessex Waste Disposal Authority
County Buildings
Casterbridge

Dear Sir

4 September 1978

Re: Application for Waste Disposal Licence at Egdon Heath, South Wessex. Ref: WDL/106/96

Talboth Friends of Wessex is a voluntary association, with over 500 local members, concerned with the protection of the environment in the Wessex area.

We wish to object to the granting of a Waste Disposal Licence at the above site, and our objections are based on the following grounds:

1. The Disposal of Waste at this site is unnecessary because of the existence of more suitable sites.

2. The Disposal of Waste at this site would cause unacceptable noise and smell to those people living in the neighbourhood.

3. The Disposal of Waste at this site would cause an unacceptable increase in heavy road traffic on all approach roads to the site.

4. Egdon Heath has been designated an Area of Outstanding Natural Beauty, and the disposal of waste at this site would greatly damage the surrounding amenitites.

5. The habitat of particular wildlife unique to this area would be severly damaged by the disposal of waste at this site.

6. While the Waste Disposal Plan for Wessex is still being formulated, it would be premature to grant a licence for the disposal of waste at this site.

Details of the above objections are attached/will be sent to you shortly, as we discussed with you.

We should, of course, be happy to supply any further information on these points, should you so wish.

Yours faithfully

Arabella Donn
Co-ordinator, Talboth Friends of Wessex

APPENDIX III

STATUTES, STATUTORY INSTRUMENTS AND CIRCULARS

The basis of United Kingdom legislation is the Statute or Act of Parliament which must pass through both Houses of Parliament and receive the Royal Assent before becoming law. In many cases the actual entry into force of a stutute is dependent on the making of a Commencement Order by the Secretary of State: this procedure being employed when administrative or other arrangements must be made or altered in order that the statute may be effectively applied. Statutes are, for reference, cited e.g. 1974 Chapter (or c. or chap.) 40.

Statutory Instruments (of which Commencement Orders are one example) include several types of documents, Regulations, Orders, Rules, Schemes etc., all of which carry the same force of law as statutes. They are sometimes referred to as delegated legislation, since they are made by, or confirmed by, the Secretary of State acting in accordance with powers established by certain provisions of many statutes. Often a statute creates a framework of law and power is then delegated to the Secretary of State to make specific regulations and orders relating to the application and administration of the framework. Statutory Instruments are mostly subject to some form of Parliamentary review or approval, but are not able to be amended by Parliament.

They are cited e.g. S.I. 1976 No. 732 or more briefly, S.I. 1976/732.

Circulars are published by Government Departments and generally consist of an explanation in layman's terms of the statute, regulations etc. to which they refer. Their main function is to explain to local authorities and similar bodies the application and administration of such statutory provisions. Circulars are cited e.g. DoE 29/78.

Statutes, statutory instruments and circulars are available from the Government Bookshop, 49 High Holborn, London WC1V 6HB, or from the branches in Edinburgh, Cardiff, Manchester, Bristol, Birmingham or Belfast, or through any good bookseller. They should also be available in most public libraries.

APPENDIX IV

WALES SCOTLAND AND NORTHERN IRELAND

Wales: The Act applies to Wales, as do all the regulations issued. But the references to public authorities in the book relate only to England, and where appropriate the following terms should be substituted.

Part I LAND:	Collection Authority:	District Council
	Disposal Authority:	District Council
Part II WATER:	Water Authority:	Welsh National
		Water Development Authority
Parts III/IV:	No change	

Scotland: The Act applies to Scotland, but different Commencement Orders and regulations apply. Contact the Scottish Office for latest details. The following terms should be substituted.

Part I LAND:	Collection Authority:	Islands or District Authority
	Disposal Authority:	Islands or District Authority
Part II WATER:	Water Authority:	River Purification Authority
Part III/IV:	Local Authority:	Islands or District Council
Throughout:	Magistrates Court:	Sheriff
	London Gazette:	Edinburgh Gazette

(for details see *s.106* of the Act).

Northern Ireland: The Act does not apply to Northern Ireland. However similar regulations to those applicable to the LAND, NOISE and WATER sections have not been issued under the Northern Ireland Act 1974. See the Pollution Control and Local Government (Northern Ireland) Order 1978 and contact the Northern Irish Office for details.

APPENDIX V

USEFUL ADDRESSES

Government Departments etc.

Ministry of Agriculture, Fisheries and Food, Whitehall Place, London SW1   01-839 7711

Department of the Environment, 2 Marsham St., London SW1 01-212 3434

Department of Transport, 2 Marsham St., London SW1 01-212 3434

Scottish Office, New St. Andrews House, St. James Centre, Edinburgh 031-556 8400

Department of Agriculture and Fisheries for Scotland, Chesser House, 500 Gorgie Rd., Edinburgh   031-443 4020

Welsh Office, Crown Buildings, Cathays Park, Cardiff 0222 28066

Department of the Environment for Northern Ireland, Parliament Buildings, Stormont, Belfast   0232 62310

Health & Safety Executive, Baynards House, 1 Chepstow Place, London W2   01-229 3456

H. M. Alkali and Clean Air Inspectorate, Beckett House, 1 Lambeth Palace Rd., London SE1 7ER   01-928 7855

Government Research Bodies

Clean Air Council, Beckett House, 1 Lambeth Palace Rd., London SE1 7ER   01-928 7855

Noise Advisory Council, Becket House, 1 Lambeth Palace Rd., London SE1 7ER   01-928 7855

Institute of Water Pollution Control, Ledson House, 53 London Rd., Maidstone, Kent   0622 62034

Clean Air Council for Scotland, Scottish Development Dept., Pentland House, 47 Robbs Loan, Edinburgh   031-443 8681 ext. 424

Water Data Unit, Reading Bridge House, Reading Berks.   0734 57551

Non-Governmental Organizations

Conservation Society, 12A Guildford St., Chertsey Surrey 09328 60975

Friends of the Earth, 9 Poland St., London W1 01-434 1684

Institution of Water Engineers & Scientists, 6/8 Sackville St., London W1 01-734 5422

National Pure Water Association, 213 Withington Rd., Manchester 061-881 5046

National Society for Clean Air, 136 North Street, Brighton, Sussex 0273 26313

Noise Abatement Society, 6/8 Old Bond St., London W1
   01-493 5877
Town and Country Planning Association, 17 Carlton House Terrace
   London SW1   01-930 8903

TABLE OF STATUTES

INDEX